The Scandal of Truth

Jean Daniélou, S.J.

translated by W. J. Kerrigan

HELICON PRESS   BALTIMORE   DUBLIN

Preface

THE SEASONS OF TRUTH

this concept that these pages are an invitation, to the sense that they may give confidence to the Christian years engaged in this mission which they have been given them, and where they must be witness of God—and, because they witness to God, servers of men.

These pages witness to a confidence in the excellence of human intelligence—created by God to know the truth—as it confronts the despair which is the attitude of so many thinkers today, even Christians. They also constitute an act of faith in the worthwhileness of existence and in man's ability to find happiness despite a world which seeks in its misery justification for revolt. They attest the worth of the created world and in particular they affirm the worth of the civilization which is developing before our very eyes. But at the same time these pages insist that the only humanism is one that accords to adoration a dimension as essential as the desire to master the world. They bear witness that while man may be destined for happiness, he has been injured by sin, and can be healed only by the Cross.

At a time when the world is searching for the insights of a new humanism, when a generation is arising eager to build a better city with the means offered by modern science, the ambition of these pages is to express these aspirations, and to give them some direction. Above all I want to say to young Christians that they should not allow themselves to be overawed by the false prestige of modern-day doctrines, whose murkiness masks the brightness of eternal truth. The shocking bankruptcy of Marxist optimism and of the philosophies of despair as well has nothing about it that should impress them. The world belongs to those who will conquer it. And it is to this conquest that these pages are an invitation, in the sense that they may give confidence to the Christian youth engaged in this mission which the world has given them, and where they must be witnesses of God—and, because they witness to God, saviors of men.

Contents

by the same author

The Dead Sea Scrolls and Primitive Christianity

Holy Pagans of the Old Testament

The Presence of God

2 THE SCANDAL OF TRUTH

CHAPTER I

The Scandal of Truth

IT WAS by no means only yesterday that truth became embarrass-
ing. The early apologist Justin Martyr had no hesitation in
seeing the trial of Socrates as a prefiguration of the trial of Jesus.
Witnesses to truth have always galled the skeptical and the
cunning. The "inhabitants of earth" seek to remove such em-
barrassments, and seeing "their corpses finally stretched on the
streets of the great city, which is called in figurative language
Sodom and Egypt, the inhabitants of earth turn to merry-making
and exchanging gifts; for the witnesses to truth had been a
torment to the inhabitants of the earth." In fact, there is no
greater stumbling block to the powerful in their schemes for
domination, and to the clever in their desire for self-sufficiency.

Thus we need not be astonished that truth has ever been hated
by the powerful, and disdained among the clever. But eventually
the sense of the truth is crippled under so many assaults, rude or
subtle, even in the souls of those who profess it. They allow
themselves to be intimidated by the kind of interrogation which
alternates mockery with menaces. They agree to relegate truth
to the dark corners of their sacristies or to the hidden places in
their hearts—and surrender to their adversaries vast areas of
intellectual activity and of civilization. At this precise moment

1

of time—our times—nothing is more seriously ailing than intelligence, nothing is less loved than truth. And so we must speak of them.

When we speak of truth, the hackles rise on many men of our day, and we can feel a defense-reaction rising in them. It is this reaction that must first be explained. How is it that to affirm the existence of truth seems to be tantamount to dogmatism and intolerance? This kind of reaction has various causes. It derives in the first place from the development of the scientific spirit. The crisis of the modern intellectual has been above all a metaphysical one, and to a great extent it still is. The certitude that ancient and medieval man thought to find in evident first principles and the deductions necessarily derived from them, the man of the eighteenth century believed he could expect from the progress of the physical sciences and of mathematics.

Many minds today still believe in this possibility. Without any doubt it remains one of the greatest obstacles to metaphysical knowledge and to acceptance of the faith. A mind that habitually associates certitude with scientific procedures is disconcerted by the techniques proper to metaphysics and to faith, and is tempted to deny them the rigor that alone elicits the unreserved adherence of the intellect. This kind of mind is willing to recognize in such metaphysical or religious affirmations the expression of sentiments to be treated with respect. But it will refuse to recognize their power to compel assent as scientific demonstrations do. This overwrought confidence in science—in the possibility that it can solve the last riddles of human destiny and free man from his last shackles—is still the state of mind of a considerable number of our contemporaries.

However, we no longer encounter this scientism among scientists. Today the difficulty brought up by the scientific mind on this question of the attainability of truth is rather the reverse.

It is less a kind of false dogmatism than a deep-rooted agnosticism. If there is one thing the scientist of today is aware of, it is the constantly provisional character of scientific systems. These systems are nothing but working hypotheses designed to express the most closely approximate interpretations of a body of known facts. And the discovery of new facts always opens up the possibility of challenging them. Now the scientist is tempted to think of this kind of knowledge as the only kind, to think that the day of dogmatic statement is definitely over and that this sense of the relative is one of the achievements of the modern mind. The notion of certitude is replaced by the notion of approximation, and an emphasis on research takes the place of an orientation towards truth.

A second reason for this crisis of truth is the low value that has come to be placed on men's word. If the scientific method of observation and experimentation is the normal way of attaining knowledge of the material world, personal testimony is the basis of all knowledge of moral realities. Our knowledge of other men depends on testimony, and so, ultimately, does our knowledge of the hidden Godhead. Testimony is a legitimate way of acquiring certitude, and even a superior way, since by testimony we can reach the very highest realities. It has its own method, too, principally concerned with the confidence to be placed in witnesses, which is the essential question of a person's word as truth.

But one of the most characteristic traits of our age is mistrust of another's word. And it must be acknowledged that this mistrust seems largely justified. The solemn word has been so much abused by the modern world as no longer to inspire trust. It is because men of today have been duped that they have become mistrustful. Every assertion puts them on guard. They have been duped by political propaganda. The finest words have covered the worst propaganda. The words of nationalism and socialism served as a screen for Hitlerite undertakings. Communist oppression labels itself democracy and pursues its plan of world domination by presenting itself as a messenger of peace. And the liberty boasted by the Free World is unfortunately often the mask for the defense of privilege.

In this sense Raymond Aron was right in showing that ours has been the age of the end of ideologies. Rather than to fine words emptied of their meaning, the young people of today are attaching themselves to the concrete realities of private life, of scientific equipment, of economic research. And political life being the pre-eminent domain of the relative and of the contingent, it is no doubt salutary to purify it in this way, as Jeanne Hirsch said, of every impure mixture of the absolute. This weariness with secular myths that transfer religious aspirations into domains that do not belong to them is quite legitimate; but, here again, in the case of many of our contemporaries, it is extended to whatever is proclaimed as true in any domain whatsoever, and in particular to assertions connected with the domain where truth has its home—the domain of the supreme values of existence and of the revelation of the living God.

There is such a thing as naive trust, and of this the man of today seems to have been quite cured. And gullibility is a disorder just as well cured, certainly. But at the other extreme is the inability to exercise considered trust even when justified by all the circumstances. And this inability seems as serious a disorder. Even among believers there often remains something deep down not completely cured of doubt, a certain inability to trust someone other than one's self which reveals some pathology, a radical weakness, a powerlessness to leave off questioning and reach the stage of assent. And, of course, there is the cautiousness about trusting another for fear of being deceived. But there is also the dread of trusting another for fear of losing one's own autonomy. And withholding one's trust in circumstances where trust is fully justified is as unreasonable as rejecting evidence when it is overwhelming. That there are many lies does not mean that there is no truth.

A third reason for the crisis of the sense of truth in the present-day world is to be found in a shift of perspectives, whereby the subjective viewpoint of sincerity is substituted for the objective viewpoint of truth. This seems to be one of the most characteristic features of modern feelings in these matters. More importance is likely to be attached to the sincerity with which a man lives a faith than to that faith's objective value. We are not denying that every sincere man deserves respect. But the sincerity with which a cause is held is really no argument for it. The worst causes have known fanatics whose sincerity has been beyond all suspicion. One can respect a man while detesting the ideas that he represents. The fact that there are sincere Communists does not justify communism. Yet such is the thinking too often met today.

Examples of it could be pointed out in many fields. For the idea of an objective morality, which consists in the conformity of one's actions to God's will, there is substituted an individual ethics, consisting of the conformity of one's actions with one's own view of things. This is what characterizes the ethics proposed by most contemporary writers, whether it be Malraux or Montherlant, Camus or Sartre. And it was Gide's ethics before them. The only duty is to realize one's self completely, whether in the line of the will to power, or in revolutionary activity, or in the night of contemplation. Malraux's *La condition humaine* is a characteristic novel with this attitude. Everyone makes his own rules for himself, and all that is required of him is to conform to them.

The same attitude is to be found in the area of religion.

More importance is attached to the genuineness of religious feeling than to the content of the faith to which one adheres. It matters little, you will be told, whether you are Buddhist, Moslem, or Christian; the main thing is that you be sincere in your belief. And here again there is a grain of truth in the argument; and it is true that men acting in good faith will be judged on the basis of their own lights. But this does not change the fact that a man can be in good faith and still be wrong, and that the presence of religious men in every religion does not make all religions equal. And the subjective consideration of the quality of religious feeling cannot outweigh the primary importance of the truth of what the mind adheres to.

Finally, we shall name one more feature of the modern world: the substitution of the criterion of effectiveness for the criterion of truth. We are not speaking simply of the warped view that the worth of ideologies is to be measured only in terms of their power to move the masses. This is again a matter of propaganda techniques, already mentioned; they are always efficient, unfortunately, but, as we have remarked, people in our day have begun to detect the cynicism behind them. What I wish to speak of is something that lies deeper, namely, the greater emphasis placed on the effective results of an action than on the principles of that action. Here again, this attitude has some justification. Too great a spectacle has been made of principles admirable in themselves, but breaking down in practice. People today judge by results. This without any doubt is one of the reasons for the attraction exercised by the "people's democracies" on undeveloped countries.

A Christian freely admits that truth is inseparable from effectiveness. Origen saw the transformation wrought by grace in men's souls as the great proof of the divine truth of Christianity. And St. Paul before him had called the Gospel "an instrument of God's power (*dynamis*), that brings salvation" (Rom. 1:16). By the same token, a Christian will admit that the Christian world has not influenced civilization as much as it might have—this not through a defect of Christian belief, which involves an inescapable requirement of charity (and of social charity), but because of the unfaithfulness of Christians. But, from the point of view that has our attention here, the danger is that of a primacy of action over doctrine, when action should be the fruit of truth, and charity the work of faith. This is unquestionably what has brought too many present-day Christians, plunged headlong into activity without sufficient preparation, without thought of what their activity is based on, to swallow many an erroneous proposition and to become the easy prey of Marxism.

* * *

If we turn now to the Bible, either the Old Testament or the New, we find ourselves confronted with an entirely different world, one where truth occupies the place of preponderant importance, and presents a very well defined content. Truth consists in the mind's giving to things the importance they have in reality. Now, the thing that is sovereignly real is God. Truth, then, must consist in the mind's acknowledging God's sovereign reality. This reality is that of God as he is in himself. Truth must consist in acknowledging God's infinite majesty and holiness. This is also the reality of God as expressed in his work. Truth, therefore, must consist in the intelligence's being conformed to the divine intelligence, to the divine sense of existence. It will consist in the will's entering into the ways of God, co-operating with his designs, and aiding him to accomplish his work in us and in the world.

But, in actuality, for the majority of men what is most real is the world of their material existence; and what is most unreal is the world of God. This is a fact so enormous, a subversion so radical and so world-engrossing that we are scarcely aware of it, and what is sin is taken for nature. This in particular is the fundamental character of a humanism which is persuaded of its self-sufficiency and takes the religious dimension to be a kind of optional accessory, entirely a matter of taste. In this view, there is possible a common ground where atheist and Christian humanists can understand each other and which each individual can extend into whatever mystical realm suits his fancy. For the Bible, in contrast, the religious dimension is the measure of man as he really is. The fact of existence puts man automatically in relationship with God. Thus it is man himself that Christianity defends when it rejects every kind of atheistic humanism as a mutilation and as a suicide.

Thus there is an order of the real where things are ranged hierarchically according to their density of existence, their weight, what St. Augustine called *auctoritas*. Truth consists in the intelligence's conforming itself to this order. Being intelligent means simply that. Intelligence does not consist in the more or less brilliant performance of the mind. No, it consists in knowing reality as it is. That is why for the Bible being intelligent means recognizing the sovereign reality of God. Who but "the fool says in his heart: There is no God" (Ps. 13:1). This is the complete reverse of what modern man calls intelligence. For in the biblical view a great intellectual may be perfectly stupid, and some poor uneducated woman praying in a church infinitely more "intelligent" than he.

Thus from the biblical perspective what first strikes us when we look at the world is this sort of lack of intelligence, this fundamental error of judgment whereby men attach so much importance to things which have no importance, to such phantoms as money, pleasure, or fame, and none to what has importance, namely, God, and his design. And surely if God really is complete value, complete holiness, complete perfection, and lovable above all things else, there is something very odd in his being so little known and so little loved. This radical upside-down situation is sin itself, sin in its ontological root, on the level of being before coming to the level of action, a sort of immense unreason, that world "out of joint" of which Hamlet spoke, that "center of wretchedness" which Péguy met in his relentless progress and which seemed to him insurmountable, like a hill too steep to climb. How is intelligence to be set aright?

But how, first of all, was such a lack of judgment ever possible? It is to precisely this question that we look to the Bible and to Christianity for an answer. For, after all, to say that sin is a lack of judgment, an error, is to say what was known to the philosophers of old. Such, particularly, was Plato's idea. To say what we have said thus far is only to affirm the belief that the mind was made for being, and that the meeting of the two is truth. And this affirmation is proper to any sound philosophy. That it is no longer taught by a number of our philosophers, that in the exercise of the intelligence they emphasize exclusively the creative spontaneity of the mind, or that they recognize objectivity only on the level of economic or biological conditioning—this proves only that they are not real "philosophers." But why such a subversion can exist is the question we must answer. And, here again, it is to the Bible that we are led, at the point where the problem of truth and error is no longer confined to the area of speculation, but touches again the tragic background of the mind's fate at the point where intelligence is touched by the mystery of evil.

And here we reach a distinction of prime importance. For Plato, the opposite of truth is error; for the Bible, the opposite of truth is a lie. A lie consists in giving an appearance of existence to what does not exist; truth consists of detaching one's self from appearances in order to adhere to reality. Now, for St. John, the devil is the father of lies; "there is no truth in him. When he utters falsehood, he is only uttering what is natural to him" (8:44). The devil is the great illusionist. He prompts us to give importance to what has no importance; he clothes with a false glitter what is least substantial; and, conversely, he turns us away from what is surpassingly real. He causes us to live in a world of seeming and of shadows. And it is the Holy Spirit, in contrast, who endears the things of God to us, who banishes falsehood, who leads us to the sovereign realities.

Thus the domain of intelligence is not excluded from the world revealed to us by the Bible, the world of the spiritual combat which takes place within man. If there is any doctrine which appears constantly and with astonishing continuity throughout the tradition of Christian anthropology it is that one. The Gospel of St. John is dominated by this conflict between the "father of lies" and him who said, "I am the way, the truth and the life." The spirituality of the Fathers, from Hermas to Athanasius, describes the tendencies of the two spirits. And in a later century Loyola was to make this distinction the key to spiritual direction.[1] But it was above all St. Augustine who showed the close connection between the quest for the Truth and conversion of the heart, and described the theological infrastructure of the intelligence's destiny.

[1] On the philosophical implications of the doctrine of the discernment of spirits, see G. Fessard, *La dialectique des exercices spirituels*, pp. 255–305.

It is in this light that we may see the real significance of the various disorders afflicting modern intelligence as we described them a few pages back. Not that they are really so modern. St. Augustine described them all through having known them all. And which of us does not know them, in the shape of those temptations which Christianity teaches us not to ignore, but to surmount.

First, there is *curiositas*, the insatiable questing of a mind which endlessly scrutinizes the visible world and its laws and conceives of every reality on the type of what is least real. For to judge that everything is relative in the realm of what is indeed relative, that is wisdom. But centuries ago Pascal—who had the right to speak, for he knew what he was speaking of—detected the error of method in the attempt to apply the spirit of geometry to the things of man, or the spirit of astuteness to the things of God. For every realm there is a corresponding "spirit." No method is exact that leaves this consideration out of account.

Worse yet is the *curiositas* which makes an object of curiosity out of what touches the serious side of life. It would be good to study the implications of the word "interesting," so characteristic of our modern vocabulary, and so apt to usurp the place of "true." Thus the pages of some of our magazines shrewdly juxtapose the life of the Trappists and the life of call girls; liturgy and strip-tease. Perhaps never has man been so curious about things religious, and perhaps never so little religious himself. The most atheistic countries are delighted to keep up inoffensive monasteries that can be shown to visitors, like reservations where the last members of some Indian tribe are to be found. Modern man is bidden to a perpetual spectacle, offered him morning, noon, and night by television, stage, and moving pictures. He knows everything. He understands everything. But in between hangs a shimmering veil which disguises everything.

Doubt is still another thing. It is that radical reserve which enables the mind to lend itself to everything, on condition that it give itself to nothing. But there is no doubt about it that one sees faith in another's word as a secret menace to one's desire to be one's own master. It is certain that trusting another means taking one's stand on some one else's intelligence and embracing as true what one has not decided for one's self. And it will be admitted that this renunciation of the reason may be reasonable. But it implies a recognition by the mind of its own limits, an acceptance of dependence, a surrender of my absolute sovereignty. It is certain that, on the level of testimony, knowledge is paired with love, for it is based on the excellence acknowledged in another, which justifies the confidence I place in him. But this confidence impinges on a certain deep-seated selfishness in me. And so once more we find that the seemingly most speculative exercise of the intelligence has a moral substructure.

And modern sincerity? It consists essentially in conformity to one's self. It means submitting to law, but a law that everyone decides upon for himself. It gives generous scope for self-esteem, since no one decides upon what does not suit his humor. The acknowledgment of a truth which does not come from me, but which is imposed upon me—not as an exterior compulsion, either, but as an excellence which commands my unconditional homage—this is infinitely more inhibiting. If the man of today rejects Christian truth, I can never be made to believe that this is through fear for his comfort, but because this truth intrudes Another into his life and because his life is thus at the mercy of that Other.

But when it comes right down to it, there is more genuineness in bearing witness to the truth, even when it condemns me, than in refusing to recognize it so that I can maintain a good conscience. Rejecting objective truth amounts to a subtle willingness to set my face against God. For—and St. Augustine witnesses to this point, too—the absolute of the truth which enlightens my intelligence is the absolute in the first instance of the Word of God.

And anyone who takes a candid view, and is not the dupe of his own rationalizations, even when he amuses himself with them, sees very well that the rejection of the truth comes down to the choice of self-affirmation and rejection of affirmation of God. For I know well enough that acknowledging what is, submitting to the real, means acknowledging something that I have not decided for myself and therefore already saying yes to God. Accepting happiness automatically means giving thanks. That is why modern man has a taste for unhappiness. Implacable fate enables one to blame God and to justify revolt. That is why for Sartre and Malraux, for Montherlant and for Camus, fate must be implacable, and the world absurd. Granted that, then my liberty flares momentarily like a lone meteorite in infinite nothing. Similarly, to accept the truth, to acknowledge what is, is tantamount to saying yes to God. That is why the mind that insists on being utterly self-dependent is complacent in falsehood, which is the one thing that an individual has totally at his own disposition. He chooses nothingness through a desire to receive nothing from anyone else: "This at least is mine, all mine," Rivière said of sin.

On the level, finally, of effectiveness, the Satanic face of the rejection of truth is finally unmasked. So long as it was only a question of sincerity, my determination to be answerable only to law of my own making concerned, finally, me alone. But on the level of the pragmatic where does the sanction come from? What becomes the norm and law now is the will of a collectivity, called self-awareness of the proletariat, genius of the race, impulse of history. In other words, what we get now instead of acknowledgment of a sovereign Law by which all will be judged, individuals and society, is the arbitrary decision of one particular will, which decrees good and evil, and against which there is no longer any appeal. It is in the name of this principle that national interests, or the class struggle, become supreme values, finding their justification precisely in their success.

Here at the end of the line the perverse roots of the rejection of truth are stripped bare. The will to power appears in all its inexorableness. What was at first tricked out as an emancipation now owns itself an escort to slavery. And it is God's Law that is now revealed as the only guarantee of liberty. In our attempted survey of modern intelligence, whose theological roots we have undertaken to show, we have now reached a kind of limit, a point where excess itself provokes its contrary. In this odyssey of the intelligence, then, perhaps we have reached the moment of a righting of the course.

* * *

Let us, in fact, now return to the present-day situation of the intelligence. It presents a strange paradox. We find on the one hand the men deputed to speak for it, to exhibit it, the pundits of the world of ideas, the philosophers. Yet I must say that on the whole their attitude towards truth seems to me to justify the deep apprehensiveness which I have just expressed. We find among them historians well equipped to conduct us through the museum of the curiosities of human thought, exhibited like dead butterflies under glass. We find among them men artful at disabusing—they tell us—young bourgeois of their naive preconceptions, at teaching them to bring everything back into question, and, finally, at leaving nothing standing but the brilliant play of their own dialectic. We find among them those for whom in all seriousness the idea of absolute truth is the enemy to be destroyed, its place to be taken by the sense of history as represented by the will of the proletariat.

I shall be told that I am severe. I think not. Of course there are exceptions, outstanding exceptions, to what I have been saying. And it is also true that meeting a school of thought contrary to one's own may serve to force one's mind to reconsider its own positions more critically. But it takes only a few minds warped, among the leaders, for irreparable damage to be done. And if there is one way in which I think academic freedom must be asserted, it is in parents' exercising their right to refuse to send their adolescent children to teachers—and in adolescents' refusing to listen to teachers—who threaten to destroy youth's most precious possession. Nor, by the way, is this to say that Christian teachers are always better. One can have faith and be perverted on the level of the intelligence. Nor is the case so rare today of those who dissociate their faith (which they set up in isolation from all the rest) from their intelligence, which they permit to be saturated with all the sophisms of their times.

Now, at the very moment when philosophers have given up believing in philosophy, there are other men who are turning towards it, men who, precisely because they are in touch with reality, are taking seriously what philosophy has to offer. I am thinking of scientific circles, where today more than ever men find themselves up against the limits of their own disciplines and where, on the other hand, the very progress of science and of its technical applications is posing problems which science itself is insufficient to solve. We have only to read the account of the problems of conscience which atomic-research scientists feel themselves faced with and we will be well aware of the importance of this matter. Because the scientist of today is in contact with reality, at the spearhead of progress, and at grips with responsibilities, he is actually on the threshold of a splendid humanism. But he is waiting for someone to help him discover its laws. It is through physics that our age will rediscover metaphysics. And that without doubt is what makes the work of a Teilhard de Chardin, even with all its deficiencies, more rich in hope and more promising in the vistas it discloses that the work of any number of philosophers bent upon the devaluation of the intelligence.

What is true of scientists is truer still of responsible leaders in economic and political life. They are receiving a dramatic revelation of the fact that technological solutions are not enough. These solutions must rest ultimately upon a conception of man. And what this conception is, it is up to others to tell them. Faced with the subversion of values represented by Marxism, they are asking for someone to show them where the values are that can ultimately justify their efforts. It is no longer ideological propaganda that they are calling for, but for something more profound, namely, for viable bases for a human order. In the mighty struggle in which the "people's democracies" and the Free World are opposed, it is neither the East nor the West that is ultimately at stake, but man himself who must be defended. Else of what earthly good are military organizations and economic programs? The indispensable thing, then, is to find out what man is, and the human person, and human liberty.

But who is to answer these questions? Who is the deputed representative of permanent values, the "shepherd of being," as Heidegger put it? The function of the philosopher in the state is beyond measure. He alone appears above suspicion. Not that it is required of him to contrive the theory of political systems and to make himself their prophet. There is no worse comedown for the philosopher than being reduced to justify political regimes, which it is his mission, instead, to judge of. Such chores we leave to Communist ideologists. The philosopher has as his mission to judge, but not to destroy. He must denounce malfeasance by reference to principles. Yet he has not this right unless he is the witness to principles. Otherwise he is a leaven of destruction. Criticism is not legitimate unless it is constructive. One has the right to judge only what one loves.

Truth here is the opposite of ideology. Ideology takes what is purely contingent and turns it into dogmatism. It makes absolutes out of economic collectivity or economic liberty. In one camp it condemns capitalism as the original sin; in the other, it finds the root of all evil in collectivism. It is, in Benda's just designation, "the treason of the learned." Men of learning are traitors when they applaud government leaders instead of daring to remonstrate with them. Truth, in contrast to ideology, is the law from which neither princes nor commoners are exempt. It is the charter of the Testament, in the name of which the Jewish prophet used to denounce the unfaithfulness of the people. But he had this right only in so much as he was the representative of the truth, and because he believed in the truth, and because he was acquainted with the truth.

At this moment of time, then, there is a divorce between the rebirth of the sense of truth among men who are not intellectuals, or at least not philosophers, and a permanent crisis of the sense of truth among numerous intellectuals, philosophers in particular. Now, this divorce is a serious matter. For men who do not find this sought-for truth among those whose mission it is to give it to them will try to find it in dogmatisms which are sometimes jerry-built and often do not distinguish between truth and ideology. But whose fault is this? We may have lately remarked the influence of integrism upon the big brass both in industry and in the military. Yet where are those who thirst for truth to look for it if the professors of thinking are no longer capable of giving it to them?

* * *

The problem is to bring about a reconciliation between the intelligence and truth. The divorce is ruinous to both. To the truth, for it must not be solely an exterior norm, imposing itself from outside upon a mind remaining passive. It is fully truth only when it is acknowledged by the mind and embraced as truth. If intelligence is something more than mental activity, truth is something more than brute reality which comes barging in, pure factitiousness of being in the Sartrian mode. Truth is the intelligence's grasp of its unison with being, and being's transparence to the mind.

This divorce is ruinous likewise to the intelligence. The intelligence has no fulfilment, as we have said, save in the knowledge of being. To be intelligent is to know that which is. By finding its complaisance in its own empty activity, it wastes itself on meaningless arpeggios; and it is not hard to understand how, tired of its pretty tricks, many people turn on it with a sort of masochistic repudiation and sacrifice it to the demands of activity.

But we believe in the dignity of intelligence. No, prostituted though she has been, we shall never repudiate her. Conversely, when we ask her to turn again to truth, it is the very opposite of a repudiation that we ask of her, for we but ask her to realize her own nature. Truth is no stranger to her. It is interior to her. It is her transparence to herself in a light more interior to her than herself—*intimior intimo meo*, said St. Augustine. And it is by being faithful to this light that she herself will become once more the light which men need to see their way by.

CHAPTER II

Truth
and
Liberty

ONE CHARACTERISTIC which contemporary humanisms have in common is their claim that freedom is sufficient unto itself and must not be assigned a subordinate place in any order. This attitude is by no means confined to philosophical tomes. And we meet it in particular in Camus or in the earlier Malraux. But the fact remains that its defenders feel that its philosophical justification is rooted in phenomenology. Our first task, then, will be to inquire whether the phenomenological method as such does imply the flat rejection of any ontology. If it does not, we shall then have to look to see where the real roots are of the humanisms which make human freedom the first and only truth.

Does existential phenomenology necessarily lead to an atheistic stand, in such a way that every representative of that school will be necessarily a denier of God? I had the opportunity to put this question personally to Maurice Merleau-Ponty, at the Geneva "Rencontres Internationales" in 1952, which he and I attended. He had delivered a talk which was at once remarkable and disquieting; and in the question period which followed I asked him whether there could be a Christian existentialism.

I take his answer from the stenographic notes as printed in the minutes of the congress:

"What I mean to say personally," said he, "is that the Pope has reason to condemn existentialism."

(I have no idea, by the way, where he got this condemnation, something new to me.)

"There are," he went on, "an enormous number of Christians who are interested in existentialism as a method, as an entrance way, as a vestibule. But as Catholics they can look on it only as a vestibule and as an entrance way, and then get back as smartly as possible to ontology in the classical sense of the word. Now, for me, this is the negation of phenomenology, of philosophy. As for those among Christians who are interested, in depth, in existentialist phenomenology—I think this is an inconsistency. One can absolutely not speak of a Christian existentialism; I think in fact that this exists—and Gabriel Marcel," he added, "is in this category—but these are individual inconsistencies. One cannot be seriously pondering the contingence of existence and still hold to the *Syllabus*."

There, then, is the very clear position of an eminent contemporary philosopher, asserting the incompatibility of a consistent existentialism and the acceptance of Christian dogmas, of which the *Syllabus* can be considered as furnishing one of the expressions. This presents us with the question: Is Merleau-Ponty entitled to settle upon this impossibility? And to answer it we must inquire into the exact nature of existential phenomenology so as to see whether it seems really bound up with a necessary denial of the absolute. To do so, we must first determine the meaning of the expressions "phenomenology" and "existentialism"; I have been using them, but with the realization that it is indispensable to explain precisely what they convey. What distinguishes the phenomenological method—as it has been employed since Husserl and above all since Heidegger, and as it has been given expression in France in the work of Sartre and Merleau-Ponty—is the determination to restrict one's self to the consideration of "phenomena," that is to say (as the parent Greek term *ta phainomena* tells us), to the study of what *appears*. This is to say that phenomenology is essentially a description of what exists (and it is by virtue of this fact that it is existential), of existence as it presents itself to us, without any question about whether this existence has any substratum or background.

This constitutes the method itself, insofar as it is a method of metaphysical analysis of the various situations in which man may find himself. But the existentialism of Sartre and of Merleau-Ponty goes in fact further than this. It undertakes to restrict itself to a description of the situation in which man finds himself. But it also undertakes to define the general properties of being. Consequently it also constitutes an ontology, a total explanation, and one that involves a novel conception of being itself. Yet, on the other hand, it asserts that the object of this ontology—of this philosophy in the formal sense—is not reducible to the phenomena described, which constitute this appearance, which in turn is the only object accessible to us; but at the same time it asserts that the object of this ontology is not something as it were hidden behind this appearance, either. In other words, existentialism as conceived by Sartre and Merleau-Ponty consists essentially in the tenet that there can be absolutely nothing else than what we can reach through awareness of the various situations in which man finds himself. Their empirical formulation—that we can reach only phenomena—is accompanied by the metaphysical tenet that nothing but phenomena can even exist. And the idea that, behind what *appears*, there might be something else, something really and truly being, not reached directly by experience, but deduced from, concluded from, supported by, asserted on the strength of, this experience—this they view as a kind of philosophical shell game, and an essential departure from the existential method.

So, there can be no being besides the one that appears, which is manifested in contingent existence. All that can be added is that this being is diversified in the variety of manifestations proper to it. According to Sartre, it is present both in the *en-soi* (that is, in the datum, as appearing to us in what Sartre calls "factitiousness") and in the *pour-soi* (that is, in the reaction of our consciousness and our liberty to that datum). But these two aspects, which make up reality, come down finally to being nothing more than two aspects of an essentially contingent world, beyond which there is absolutely no absolute for us to look for. Reality is thus a perpetual creation, absolutely unpredictable, which results from the reaction of our freedom with the various situations with which it finds itself confronted.

In view of this position, we are confronted not simply with a method of description of the various situations within which man can find himself, but with the assertion (one, then, strictly on the philosophical plane) that this is the only thing that exists and that nothing else even can exist. We see very easily, that is, that Sartre and Merleau-Ponty pass from a method of describing reality to a metaphysical assertion on the content of all reality. For what makes a metaphysics is nothing more nor less than an assertion about being itself, that is to say the ultimate basis of things. In asserting that the ultimate basis of things is never anything but this contingent existence, and that there exists nothing besides this world in the variety of its manifestations—that this is the only reality that exists or can exist—in so doing, our authors are on a metaphysical plane.

This constitutes, in effect, as already remarked, and here again we are employing precisely the language used by this school, the transition of a philosophy from an existential method, that is to say from a description of existence in the variety of its aspects, to an existential philosophy, which is to say practically to a new metaphysics. As Jean Wahl in his *Histoire de la philosophie de l'existence* has well remarked, these philosophers have started, with Kierkegaard, the great pioneer in this enterprise, from a study of existence properly so called in terms of a concrete datum made the subject of description, and ended up with a new metaphysics—a metaphysics of the contingent, involving the existence of the contingent only, on the basis of the elaboration of the idea of existence.

But this, undeniably, constitutes a step beyond the method we described at the outset. And so we are brought to make this comment, of capital importance for what we have to say, namely, that it is not the phenomenological method as such, and in itself, which goes contrary to the affirmation of a God and the recognition of the absolute; no, it is instead a specific ontology, a specific metaphysics, superimposed upon the phenomenological method by Sartre and Merleau-Ponty. And one may even wonder whether this new ontology, shutting up man in his contingence, is not a return to precisely what the first existential philosophers—and I am thinking here of Kierkegaard in particular—undertook to set the philosopher free from. We may wonder, that is, if it does not bring us back to a positivism, a rationalism which is the very thing Kierkegaard took up his position against, violently protesting against the insufficiency of the brute fact, and championing, conversely, in the name of the ineluctable requirements of existence, an ultimate meaning to things—an absolute. The Russian philosopher Shestov's is the genuine existentialism, holding the world of contingence, in which we are shut up by pure experience, to be a prison, a prison that we can escape from. Sartre and Merleau-Ponty, it may be said, inclose us again in the prison from which it was precisely the aim of the first existentialist philosophers to free us.

We must go still further in our criticism and say that even on the level of phenomenological description, of the description of man-on-the-spot, objections can be brought against Sartre and Merleau-Ponty. For one thing, the latter insists a great deal on what he calls ambiguity: ambivalence of soul and body, which are two merely dialectical aspects of one and the same reality; ambivalence of good and evil, which are not opposed as two contradictory realities, but each in fact being always more or less implied by the other. True enough, in the rejection of abstract analyses is to be found one of the elements that give existential analysis its value. Existential analysis is correct in refusing to attribute to complex reality the abstract divisions which are the work of the mind. And, to be sure, it is pure gain for the phenomenological method to place us always in the presence of certain *totalities,* of a unit, that is, comprising complex attitudes, bound one to another, which we must grasp thus in their togetherness.

I shall be giving examples of this in a moment. But the point must be brought up that one of the most noteworthy features of phenomenological analysis, particularly as practiced in its early days by Husserl and Max Scheler, was its revealing that certain data of human experience, which an attempt had been made to explain in terms of one another, were not in fact thus reducible.

Of this I shall cite some examples at once. Max Scheler, in his book on the nature and forms of sympathy, in reaction against certain sociological and certain psychoanalytical explanations of love, showed that between the infectious emotion that pervades a crowd galvanized by some orator, sexual love, and spiritual love, there exist not simply differences of degree, permitting a sliding on the scale from one to another, but, in sober fact, radically distinct essences. Similarly Otto, in his book on the idea of the holy, shows us that religious situations, where man is in contact with the absolute, are of such makeup as is absolutely irreducible to a sublimation of affectivity or to group-generated tension. In other words, there are data of human experience that cannot be reduced to one another. What if phenomenology does simply stop at this descriptive stage? This is already a considerable achievement; and I for my part think that one of the essential features of phenomenology is its protest against the intolerable reductions of this kind that nineteenth-century positivism used to make so often.

In reality, Merleau-Ponty reintroduces dialectic—the continual movement from one reality to another, each demanding the other. But if dialectic, as Father Fessard has shown, is a proper instrument for the analysis of historical situations, which present us with factors that are complementary, it is no fit instrument of analysis in the metaphysical order. In Hegelian and Marxist dialectic there is therefore something radically vitiated, in that their dialectic rests on the notion of a certain total homogeneity of realities one with another, whereas existentialism for Kierkegaard, in reaction against Hegel and Hegelian dialectic—and it must never be forgotten that it was essentially against Hegel that Kierkegaard took his position—was precisely an assertion of the radical distinction of orders (in Pascal's sense of the word) and of the irreducibleness in particular of the absolute to the various aspects of contingent existence.

Still another criticism may be brought against atheistic existentialism for privileging certain situations at the expense of others, and for identifying phenomenology, as a description of existence, with the description of the atheist existentialist's *own* existence. From this point of view a Gabriel Marcel, a Christian existentialist, rightly protests against Sartre, when Sartre privileges certain situations like nausea, that is, the disgust a man experiences on confronting the abyss of his freedom, and when he refuses, in contrast, to consider that hope may constitute an existential situation just as genuine. In fact, the phenomenological method as such does not permit the making of value-judgments that sanction the privileging of one kind of situation at the expense of some other. From this point of view a phenomenology of belief is possible alongside a phenomenology of unbelief. I mean that the believer will come up with a phenomenology of faith, while the unbeliever will come up with a phenomenology of absence of faith. Consequently it may be asserted that there is indeed a shell game in the atheistic existentialists' claim that phenomenology leads necessarily to a justification of atheism, whereas this is simply the expression of their own particular situation in existence.

I shall offer another example of this from the debate I had with Merleau-Ponty. In that debate, Merleau-Ponty had explained that it is the property of language to afford us an opportunity to invent, and that what is interesting in the realm of language is novel statement: the new combinations to which language lends itself. In the discussion that followed I pointed out to him that scope for novel invention may be one aspect of the value of language, but that the fact of being able also to conserve what has been said, and which has abiding validity, may be considered a quite as essential function of language. I pointed out that the fact, for example, that what was said by Plato, and what was said by Shakespeare, have been preserved for us—not to speak of the special case of language's having preserved for us what was said once and for all by Jesus Christ —may be considered a more important function than the combinations which the Surrealists are able to arrive at by arranging words in some undreamed-of order. In such a case as this, Merleau-Ponty was privileging one category, invention, as against another category, transmission. But we can give him the direct reply that invention and transmission are two situations of language which are both perfectly valid, and that there is no reason to privilege one of these functions in relationship to, and in opposition to, the other.

One particular case in this business—one involving a basic consideration in the judgment we have to pass on existentialism —is that of a person's relationship with other people. In the situation, as described by existentialist phenomenology, the other person is a prime datum. This is, to be a man is to be in the world, and this being-in-the-world implies that man is a being in relationship with other beings. And indeed one may say that this is one of the achievements of phenomenology. The problem for certain philosophers is to manage to find something other than themselves, once having taken themselves as their point of departure, whereas phenomenology puts us quite out of the way of that danger: it is in that regard the very opposite of a subjectivism or a solipsism.

Nevertheless, in connection with this "other people" which is a prime datum of existence, Sartre, and I am thinking here particularly of him, brings back in precisely the old opposition between subject and object, which it was the very purpose of existentialism to set us free from. In the measure that other people, for Sartre, are part of the *en-soi*, that is, part of the datum of brute fact, which we run up against, to that extent other people, for Sartre, are objects. No work of Sartre's is more characteristic of this attitude than *Huis clos,* which presents us exactly with the impossibility of communication with other people. *"Hell,"* says Sartre in this play, *"is they."* Other people, that is, make up that prison which we run up against: we try to make objects of them, but without achieving any communication. Sartre thus re-establishes a solitude of the individual face to face with the world, a solitude which is not here the solitude of a subjective idealist, but the solitude of the opposition between a subject and a world entirely opaque to his penetration.

But this is in no way implied by phenomenological analysis as such. And, taking the same point of departure, a Gabriel Marcel constructs, in contrast, a philosophy of communication, which is doubtless the feature of his philosophy to which he holds most strongly, and in which the initial indetermination, between self and other people, is developed into a philosophy of intersubjectivity, that is, communciation among subjects, which for Gabriel Marcel is the very expression of the indubitable existential; that is, the absolutely basic datum, love, inasmuch as it is communication with other people, appears as the absolutely indubitable reality, which I cannot place in doubt, and the basis on which every metaphysics can be erected.

We may note the value a contribution like that one may have for a Christian philosophy as metaphysical justification of a theology of charity. But it is equally valuable for a concrete philosophy of knowledge. The knowledge afforded by faith is a knowledge which comes about in intersubjectivity. That is, it is of the essence of knowledge acquired by faith to be received by transmission through witnesses. And that is precisely what is sometimes irritating to present-day minds, in that they wish to reach all truth on their own. Now, knowledge achieved by faith forces us to acknowledge that on the level of the essential certainties of existence—that is, relating first of all to our knowledge of others, and eminently to our knowledge of God—love and intelligence become indissoluble; here we must acknowledge, that is, that we depend necessarily upon one another in the discovery of truth. It is therefore together, and only together, that we can have access to the truth which is fundamental.

Now there is no reason why Sartre's position, which considers other people to be an object, should be a more legitimate application of the phenomenological method than Marcel's position, which considers other people to be, on the contrary, a subject. These are two interpretations of the initial data, interpretations of which one can say at the very least that either is quite as legitimate as the other, so that there is no reason to privilege Sartre's judgment of the data over Marcel's, and that only metaphysics will enable one to render a decision.

Thus these various remarks have led us to make a radical distinction between existential phenomenology's method of analysis and the use which certain existentialists today make of it in order to draw negative conclusions regarding the claims for an absolute. We may say that phenomenology as such is in no way bound up with the denial of God, and is not dependent on any determinate ontology. Likewise, it is susceptible to various utilizations. There is that which a Sartre, a Merleau-Ponty, and others give it; but there is also—and it seems to me very important to remember this—an existentialism examples of which we meet when it comes to Catholics, like Marcel and Guardini, or Jews, like Martin Buber, or an Orthodox like Lev Shestov.

We come now to the question, since existential phenomenology does not in itself lead to a denial of God, what is it that brings atheistic existentialists, and in particular those of whom we are speaking, to deny the existence of an absolute? They do not do so, let it be said, through any requirement on the part of their existentialism; they do so, therefore, in virtue of a certain philosophy, a certain metaphysics, which they thus add on to the phenomenological method itself. Now, if we examine all their works, we may submit that their reaction to this problem is always the same. The position taken by Sartre is well known. Essence does not precede existence. This means that, for Sartre, it is the decision of my liberty which is, at each moment, the absolute beginning. It is not commanded, determined, or ruled by anything; it is, really, absolute possibility and total novelty. Man does not exist unless he is thus, by himself, the cause of his own existence. In the preface to his study of Descartes, Sartre expressed it clearly: what he did was to transfer to man what traditional philosophy attributed to God, namely, aseity, which is to say the fact of depending only upon himself.

It is at that point, too, that Sartre's humanism reaches its limit. Confronted with the abyss of his own liberty, man is seized by a sort of vertigo. This is nausea. So, for example, in *Huis clos,* are the three characters shut up in themselves, one another's mutual hell, face to face eternally with one another, each incapable of communicating with the others, and seeking in them only a looking glass in which to be mirrored. This eternal face-to-face becomes for man an intolerable hell. And it is at this point that he seeks, through a revulsion, to be freed from himself. Anything at hand is valid for this purpose. Here is the explanation of why certain intellectuals, of whom the very opposite might have been expected, have turned to communism. It explains why what has attracted them in communism has been precisely what was most at odds with themselves, namely, renunciation of liberty. Of this Dostoievsky probably had a presentiment in his legend of the "Grand Inquisitor."

Freedom is intolerable to men—they are delivered from it by slavery. Malraux once showed this perfectly in his character Vologuine in *La condition humaine*. But he has long since opened up more promising roads. Sartre, in contrast, is still taking this position today; his latest book, *La critique de la raison dialectique*, is a faithful echo of a certain French intelligentsia: "I never get anywhere; my ideas do not enable me to construct anything; so, there is no solution but Marxism." To put it in other words: My liberty, at bottom, is worthless; I shall profit by it so long as I have it; but I look for the swipe of the broom that I have coming to me.

Here is a shocking expression met rather often, even on the lips of people among whom it is astonishing to hear it: "That's what it will have to come to." Such, at the end of Tibor Mende's book, is the expression of an aged Chinese. I know people who, speaking of certain foreign lands, say: "It will be very sad, but that's what it will have to come to." This mood is an outrage—it proves that we have given up on being able to bring the world what it is looking for. It is ignoble—I abuse freedom so long as I have it, but I know the liberty I am abusing is something worthless, something I deserve to be disembarrassed of. It is a liberty that I consider blameworthy; whence the bad conscience of so many of the intellectuals of our country, who are guilty, who know it, and who await the last judgment and the hell they have merited, under the form of a "people's democracy" as their government.

What Sartre also witnesses to, and rightly so, is liberty's incapability of being sufficient unto itself. His error lies in believing that it can escape its impotence only by denying itself. The question to be determined is whether there exists any order to which liberty can commit itself without renouncing its nature. Now, that order does exist. It is a system, first of all, of reciprocity among persons. For submitting to my liberty's being limited by another person's liberty is not a renunciation of my liberty, but a recognition that I ought to be as desirous of scope for another person's liberty as I am when it comes to my own. In other words, this is transcending the level of having and reaching the level of being. Moreover, this order in which my liberty reaches self-fulfilment is according to God's plan, and is answerable not to an impersonal and extrinsic law, but to the acknowledgment of an infinitely holy personal liberty, one bound up, moreover, with the implications of my personal existence themselves, so that in obeying it I am at the same time fulfilling myself. It is in this truth that liberty has its sole realization.

CHAPTER III

The
Myth
of
Unhappiness

IT WOULD be interesting to trace the genealogy of the humanism we are speaking of. Doubtless the line would be traced back to Nietzsche. In the revolt of the creator of Zarathustra against all order there is an undeniable grandeur. But Nietzsche was the first to affirm that it is upon the death of God that man is to be reared. In this he defined very well the attitude which we are examining. Towards God, Nietzsche experienced a kind of jealousy. He submitted unwillingly to having to acknowledge a greatness which he himself could not possess. It was in him that atheism found its really positive expression, the position that man does not exist unless his excellence is supreme. What Nietzsche also saw clearly is the strict connection between God and an objective morality. He was the first representative of situation ethics. He saw clearly that morality is inseparable from God, that it is not an abstract law, but the expression of a personal will. And his transmutation of values consisted in substituting a moral system which he gave to himself for one received from someone else.

This attitude has reappeared in a number of writers and philosophers. I shall cite one of the most striking examples, Malraux's *La condition humaine*. There we find the quest (it is one character's line in the book) of life itself and of the suffering at the bottom of it, that is, a certain basic experience in the metaphysical line, which is existence itself. The characters look for it in different directions. It is in the act of killing that Tchen discovers a wholeness of selfhood that he tries to define as ecstasy. Similarly—and the thing is rather striking because the character in certain ways might seem to be possessed of a different perspective—Clappique, at the moment when he stakes all the money he has left, experiences an intensity of existence which one of the characters has spelled out. The folly of these solutions is not the important thing: They are the expression of a kind of fulness of the moment of time, an intensity of existence which has the appearance of the supremely worth while. What gives the book its interest is that the characters live in it intensely. There is not a one of them who is lukewarm. Even unsympathetic characters like Ferral have a certain greatness. In Malraux's mind, he finds in his will to power an affirmation of himself.

The world of Malraux is a world from which mediocrity is absent, where the thing is to live dangerously. Stretching towards the fulness of freedom and not being able to reach it, that is the main point. Success is devoid of interest, either on the personal level or on the political level; the worst blunder the unfortunate pastor makes is to speak to Tchen of happiness. Malraux's characters are not looking for happiness; they are looking for fulfilment. That is why it is noteworthy that the fact that their fate leads to catastrophe does not prevent them from fulfilling themselves. Quite to the contrary; should they succeed at politics or at love, that would only mean being sentenced for life to be middle class. Unhappiness is indispensable in showing that they look for nothing from fate, but that, quite to the contrary, it is to the extent that their fate is more tragic that it is revealed as better than the only thing they are looking for, namely, self-transcendence. Success is trifling; the important thing is to have been great. We may note in this connection an episode in which Malraux attains mythic power, the episode where we see Kyo's fate balanced on that little ball rolling on the gaming table. One gets the impression here of a kind of extraordinary contrast between the absurdity of a fate dependent on a trifling event and the one thing of consequence, which is one's attitude towards fate.

It seems on the other hand that every time Malraux's characters try to give a justification for their attitude, to talk either about a cause, or about an ideal, or about some reason for living, the words ring false. I shall give some examples. When, in the courtyard, Kyo before he dies is expressing what his ideal has been, he ends with a line crass enough to be the final line in a B moving picture: "The thought of me will live on at least, in the memories of men." When Gisors explains his more or less Indian philosophy, in which he expresses a vague reconciliation of personal existence with the universal, we are equally abashed. The more awesome Malraux's attitude in the presence of existence is, the more disappointed we are every time he essays a response to life on the metaphysical level. There is a disproportion between a certain attitude towards life and any justification thereof. Malraux's characters do not die for a cause; the causes are a pretext for dying; they seek death, so as to reach the dark heart of existence. This is no political gambit. All the political causes turn out, I think, to be ultimately secondary to what the characters are really seeking.

Is this, however, to say (and this is my third point) that there does not exist in the novel a certain ethics? I believe we find in Malraux a pervasive sense of virtue, and of the virtues, in Corneille's understanding of the term. And his characters are in many ways animated by genuine virtues. We find for example a certain camaraderie and humane brotherhood, a code of dignity expressed rather paradoxically in the note of truest humanity, on the part of Valery when confronted with Ferral. In addition the characters are continually offering us the example of an extraordinary courage. Unquestionably there is in all this a human grandeur rarely attained. But it is here that I come to what from the Christian viewpoint is a grave matter, where we are confronted with some real problems. Malraux's case is different from Sartre's. It is certain that Sartre's ethics have nothing that is liable to fool or deceive us. We are too much aware of all that is unacceptable in them. In contrast, Malraux's ethics, because they do reach certain heights, present us with a genuine problem. The ideal of his characters, in their asserting a kind of richness of life divorced from all the conventions, has about it something that may seduce us.

Now, this attitude has its existence on a strictly human plane, and on the plane of man's relations with man. It not only ignores, but fiercely rejects, anything which would come along and contaminate this unadulterated humanity, which, precisely, is the only thing worth man's undivided quest. So, anything like the presence of God, or relationship with a religious life, would seem like an adulterant to genuine humanity. The world of Malraux, as exhibited in *La condition humaine,* seems to be a world deliberately shut off from God, a world carefully confined to the determination to make of the relations of man to man the supreme value. Now, this seems to me what represents, today, the essential temptation, that of a certain social humanism, the temptation, not to do evil, but to show that one has no need of God in order to do good—that is, in short, to show that man is perfectly capable by himself of reaching veritable greatness, and that he has nothing to look for from God.

It is highly characteristic of this outlook that, if Malraux's heroes live in a climate of human virtues, they live in the total absence of what I shall call grace in the Christian sense of the word. They are great, yet are in the state of mortal sin. We find in them a total dissociation between an ethics corresponding to certain summits of human dignity, and Christian moral values. Each character has some variety of cockle sown in with his greatness. Gisors is an opium addict, and his addiction is an integral part of his characterization. Valerie is a demimondaine. In Tchen we find an appetite for bloodshed and killing; in the other characters, for eroticism. There is something deeply disturbing here in the very climate of the book, in the expression of this total dissociation of moral greatness from spiritual grace and from the Christian evangelical ideal. Someone cited Malraux as saying: God can die without anything's being changed. What seems to me, precisely, is that for Malraux God is dead— and that everything is changed. I believe that the ethics proposed to us by Malraux is one profoundly affected by the fact that for his heroes God is indeed dead, an ethics that quite departs from the one which we—since we think it the only one where man can reach full self-realization—still hold to.

I shall conclude by inquiring just where we may say Malraux takes up his position. It seems to me—and I am returning here to what I said at the outset—that we find in Malraux the ideal of a tragic greatness which is its own reason for being. "The martyr who has no faith" is Montherlant's expression in *Port-Royal*. What we find is a martyr who endures a torment not justified as the means to a redemption, but seeming in itself the supreme degree of greatness because it is the basic torment: the torment of existing, but not for any further purpose. Liberty is the supreme goal in an absurd world where it is ever doomed to disappointment. Malraux's position seems to me to coincide with Sartre's on the metaphysical level, though differing from it on the level of moral sensibility. Malraux is right in condemning the bondage of a society which bullies man and blocks his self-fulfillment. But where he, too, is wrong is in failing to inquire whether there is an order to which man can commit himself without destroying himself, and whether there is no possibility of liberty's making room for love and hope.

But it must also be observed that it is not the absurdity of the world which causes the revolt here; it is the revolt which introduces absurdity into the world in the first place, so as to have something to justify itself; the writers we have been discussing need evil in order to revolt; for pessimism is the indispensable diet of revolt. What comes first is the will to rebel; because these writers already want to say "no" to the world in the first place, because they already itch to bring creation to the bar, because they already want to refuse to acknowledge that the world is good, and is the work of God, and because they clutch at any and every reason they can find for rejecting his creation—that is why we find their rebellion fabricating pessimism, trying to be affronted, always giving prominence to the seamy side, looking carefully away from all that might prove of sound value, so that they may contrive to utter the "no" they have in their craw.

But, it will be objected, are we not dismissing as trifling what the world does present in justification of revolt? In an absurd world, revolt is the only way left. It is freedom's last refuge. His refusal to resign himself to his lot is the very mark of man's greatness. On that score revolt is the badge of as many Christians as non-Christians. Look for the great rebels of the modern world among Rimbaud, Nietzsche, and Camus, and you will also find Dostoievsky, Bloy, Bernanos—all who, as Peguy's Joan of Arc puts it, "are not resigned to anything." Among minds so different there is a certain family resemblance, enabling us to identify them collectively as rebels. Yet on closer view the resemblance tends to dissolve in differences.

There is an ambiguity in revolt. And this is the fact overlooked when one insists on considering revolt in the pure state. Revolt means, of course, saying "no." But everything depends on what we say "no" to. At an early stage the "no" is uttered against injustice. Revolt and justice are correlative terms. The expression of revolt is already to be found in the child who, with fists clenched and in impotent rage sees punishment dealt to someone who does not deserve it. There is the root of revolt in many cases. It is the result of the accumulation of mute indignation at the sight of "right perfection wrongfully disgraced," of what deserves to be respected and loved being misprized. It is swollen by the spectacle of social injustice or political oppression. It becomes revolution when it wakes to awareness a commonwealth of the revolted who are determined to burst their chains.

This revolt is sacred. But Camus has taught us to see that it falls short. What depends on man is limited. There is no hoax more evil than letting men think that they can install a kingdom of God on earth. By turning their heads towards the illusory historical solution, one simply takes their attention from their real tasks. You can do only a certain amount of good for people, but that little bit, at least, you can really do. This modest social responsibility which, in sum, is offered by the work of Camus, inexorably denouncing utopian ambitions, knowing that there are programs of instituting justice which commonly serve as a pretext for terrors of every kind and that the crimes of the doctrinaire are the most dangerous of all—this is the truest expression of revolt within the limits of the temporal condition of man.

Yet to say so much clearly brings us only to the threshold of the problem. For the injustices upon which man has seized are, after all, limited. The real revolt breaks out on the level of what man has not come to grips with and which he knows, if he is sane, that he cannot come to grips with. No revolution, no amount of scientific progress will ever change the scandalous fact that little children die, that good people are persecuted, that whole populations find themselves hurled into wars. And even if human effort could abate these evils, the fact would remain that they did once exist. Because of the scandal of the suffering of the innocent the word stands convicted, and revolt is justified.

This scandal is something we cannot be rid of. The world as it stands is unjust, we must own. All the brilliantly reasoned solutions, Christian or atheist, are, when it comes to this, nugatory. Never can we be made to swallow the rationalist optimism of Condorcet or of Marx, of Bossuet or of Teilhard de Chardin. Nothing is worse, when it comes to this point, than to undertake to justify God. The result will be only apologetics that will provoke loss of faith. For they are explanations that all too clearly will not square with the facts. If we had to judge things according to the norms of our justice, Camus would be right in citing God before the bar of human justice, in convicting him by due process, and in passing inexorable sentence upon him. For it is plain as day that, if justice consisted in the distribution of temporal weal and woe according to merit, the world which we know would have nothing in common with it.

But in the presence of this injustice, which must, as the first step, be acknowledged, there is the revolt of Nietzsche, and there is the revolt of Kierkegaard. Kierkegaard recognized that the world does not square with what we call justice. But he appeals from it to another justice. Kierkegaard's faith is faith in hidden ways the wisdom of which is greater than ours. And perhaps it is better so. When we see what men make of the world when they organize it by their lights, we may well wonder whether it is not preferable after all for somebody else to be pursuing a design in it that is hidden from us, but where through the chinks in the mystery provided by suffering and joy, death and life, we glimpse greatness. The world as it is gives scope for only two attitudes: revolt and faith. Faith does not exculpate the world for us. On the contrary, it presupposes scandal, for it consists in surmounting scandal.

But this act of faith, this cry raised by man, captive and powerless to free himself, for a release at the hands of somebody else—this is exactly what the revolter will have none of. Only here, we must watch out for the fact that revolt has altered in meaning. It no longer means revolt against injustice. That kind, as we have made clear, we are taking for granted. Here we are talking of revolt against dependence. It is not injustice that is being said "no" to, but the sovereignty of God. Revolt is refusal to obey. And here is the meaning of the word which is without doubt deepest—and murkiest. Everything up to this point was rejection of evil. But here revolt is the cause of evil. Evil and injustice appear here under the flag of revolt. The pure, the original, the master revolt was the revolt of the angel, poison root from which all evil stems and which pokes up perpetually the mystery of evil which enhedges us—and from which Christ alone can deliver us.

Now, the more revolt—in the prior sense of the word—appears as the expression of the greatness of man, the more (I must say, since I sense this in my whole being) it seems to me in the latter sense the expression of his paltriness. It brands the spirit incapable of the sovereignly noble disposition of the heart—adoration, which is the capacity to recognize greatness even where one does not possess it one's self. Now this capacity is the true stamp of generosity of soul. This it was that gave their incomparable qualities to Dante and to Shakespeare, to Claudel and to Bernanos, to John of the Cross and to Pierre de Berulle. In contrast, this revolt in the second sense characterizes the being who is centered upon himself, who views all things as something to own. Nietzsche gave it voice: he was jealous of Christ, restive under the obligation of acknowledging in another a greatness beyond his own means.

Now this comes down to two attitudes against which I feel my whole being protest. Either it is an absence of the sense of God, a kind of defective spiritual vision—and this is to have something missing in one's makeup. (When one realizes the almost insupportable weight of divine glory, that overwhelming and marvelous density of existence, ignorance of it seems like disability and destitution.) Or else it is outright sacrilege, the urge to trample on what is sacred. And this seems to me, I must say, something quite as vile as trampling on the rights of man. My sympathy goes to this misprized God. I feel jealous for his sake.

Thus we had reason to declare that injustice is not the cause of the revolt we meet today, but that revolt is prior and seeks justification in the absurd. And this is why we challenge the connection between greatness and unhappiness. We contend, on the contrary, that happiness is the heroic vocation of man. It is but an absurd prejudice that moves certain of our contemporaries to profess to despise it and to allow no greatness save tragic greatness. Far from being attended by ease and comfort, happiness is a difficult conquest. It is no restful haven to which one retires through weariness and debility, but adventure upon adventure braved by those who will brook no arrest. Admittedly, it has its own traps, and is open to abuse as well. Indeed, certain careers become engulfed in selfish types of happiness. And yet are we really speaking of happiness here? Are there not apparent successes which do not succeed in bestowing it? They may have a façade masking a soul that is at peace with nothing. And the very greatest spiritual successes may spring forth from the very heart of failure.

In reality, if modern man pretends to disdain happiness, he often does so because he has rendered himself incapable of it in the first place. By selling himself short, he comes to think that it would be impossible for him, and loses even the appetite for it. And that is the bottom of the abyss. If we would save men, the first thing we must do is restore at least their desire for salvation and their confidence that it is something possible for them. But here we run up against their secret complicity with nothingness and with death. And this complicity is, at bottom, the expression of a determination to be one's own master. For every mind in the least lucid recognizes that there is no happiness but implies acceptance and gratitude. It takes a good deal of humility to agree to be happy. And pride needs unhappiness to feed its rebellion. It affects to shy from happiness as a prison because it lacks the courage to face what it implies.

The hide-and-go-seek between happiness and man is a strange game indeed. Happiness hides itself from those who pursue it, and tags the players who are not looking for it. Like the Spirit, it breathes where it will. The ancients identified it with Fortune, the capricious. And the wisest of them counseled against placing trust in it. Admittedly one sure way never to be disappointed is never to expect anything. Yet that wisdom, too, falls short. For happiness is man's vocation. It is better to suffer and not renounce happiness than to find peace by renouncing it. The man of courage is the man who continues to believe in happiness despite all failures and all disappointments. And, in the end, happiness will never fail to show such a man its true face.

For happiness, when all is said and done, does not lie in having this or that, but in the discovery of the meaning of existence and in communion with the absolute. Sadness lies in disharmony, in being pulled in too many directions. It overtakes us when we no longer know where we are. It broods over desires that are torn this way and that, over a heart sundered like tumbling quicksilver. Unity is the haunt of happiness, which dwells in the depths of the heart, in a sanctuary unaccessible, where it is never at the mercy of anything. It is, down underneath the miscellany of life's occurrences, their secret unity, binding our days each to each in a vocation, the fundamental harmony of existence and its progress towards the absolute of God.

Men are mistaken in setting duty and happiness apart. Secret pride is what brings them to think that duty is purer when it looks for no recompense. There is a residue of Jansenism in this, to which the French are more prone than other folk. Montherlant granted that what attracted him in *Port-Royal* was that for him the supreme greatness is suffering. Claudel, who (for his part) believed in happiness, was right in denouncing this masochism. For God wills our happiness. He asks us to let him make us happy. The assertion of the ultimate coincidence of goodness and happiness, liberty and fate, is the fundamental cry of human existence in the face of all the seeming contradictions. This holds true, not only for the life hereafter, but for our present life.

The mistake many people make is identifying happiness with certain moments of their lives and doubting its capacity to stand the test of time. They would like time to have a stop at certain perfect moments of life, seeing in the clock that tells the time a menace to their fragile joys. Happiness is for them the paradise lost forever in the past. Now nothing is more mistaken than this. For the various happinesses with which life is visited and which are graces from God have no purpose but to awaken a taste for happiness that time alone can deepen, divest it of its trappings, strip it of what is unessential. And after having brought us to love God in his gifts, it brings us to love him for himself.

CHAPTER IV   # Poetry
and
Truth

OUR TASK—and we think it is one of the essential tasks, the essential task of our day—is a task of demystification: that is, of pointing out that there is no mysticism save that belonging to God. There is a marxist mystification which sets up revolution as a religion. Is or was. There is the mystification of scientism, looking for all salvation from evolution. There is also a poetic mystification, that is, a pretension on the part of poetry to constitute a mysticism. It is this poetic mystification which it is our business to denounce here. And doing so is doubtless the only way to free poetry from the crisis it is passing through and to enable it to find again its genuine relationship with the sacred.

Here is our contention. For the past century and a half poetry has been taken for a religion, for *the* religion. The cause for this is to be sought in the arcana of romanticism, or rather of pre-romanticism, that mysterious threshold where in Blake and Hölderlin the neo-paganism of Winckelmann joined the esotericism of Boehme, and was expressed in France in those two fragments separated by the blade of Robespierre: Chénier and Nerval. For if Chénier was not yet Nerval, Nerval was still Chénier.

49

Je pense à toi, Myrto, divine enchanteresse.

But he surpassed him. In him the formal beauty of paganism, which classicism had drawn up from its shadowy abysms, became again a religion. Poetic chant became an incantation. Woman was for him, Thierry Maulnier was to say, as she would be for Baudelaire, as she had been for Novalis, "a darkling flash in the boundless night."

Baudelaire was to enter more deliberately upon the exploration of artificial paradises. He was to remain the prince of the poets of night as defined in a remarkable page of Claudel's. The shadow of the black angel hovered over all his work. And poetry became the liturgy of this office of the dark. It became magic, incantation summoning up lost paradises by the power of the Word and opening the portals to heavens unknown. It was theology in the negative, not in the sense of the Dionysiac and Eckhartian superessence, but in the sense of the Satanic refusal to adore. The poetic act assumed a demiurgic value, setting up its absurd and ephemeral creation as a protest against the staggering weight of the glory of the divine creation.

But in Baudelaire the esoteric tradition was disengaged from the cult of pagan beauty. It was mingled with a sensibility at once pessimistic, Christian, and Jansenistic, the origins of which have been demonstrated recently. It was not until Rimbaud appeared that Nerval's ambition attained its limit and that poetic activity was asserted as an act of absolute knowledge. In it eternity was regained:

> *C'est la mer mêlée*
> *avec le soleil.*

It was brought in the *Illuminations* to its highest point of incandescence. It burnt itself out. And that is why Rimbaud was thereafter to contribute nothing to the fortunes of the time but shabby castoffs. He no longer had any sense for any who thought to reach eternity in a moment of time. Poetic activity also revealed in Rimbaud a revolutionary and subversive character, related to terrorist activity. And it is not without reason that the surrealists who inherited it have continued it in the direction both of suicide and of communism.

When it comes down to it, Rimbaud was the only poet who took Nietzsche's Death of God seriously and tried to set up experimentally a mysticism of Man as the absolute. It was he who succeeded in giving poetry its character of mystification. That is why his contentions are of direct concern to the theologian. He squared a mysticism against a mysticism. Or rather, he turned the one and only mysticism from its object in order to shunt its charge of absolute over to poetic activity. The surrealists were to be his direct heirs, beyond Apollinaire and St-John Perse. Among them poetry was to continue to be a dangerous adventure, constantly skirting suicide with Crevel, and madness with Artaud. In Breton, it was to acquire kinship with experiences of the most disquieting sort. It is in this sense that one must understand the words of Claudel, who saw in him a mystic without God, when Claudel referred to a mysticism that dispenses with God instead of obscurely seeking him. Here Etiemble is right.

One sees here the exceptional importance of Rimbaud. He tried to make poetic activity the mysticism of atheistic humanism. And this is the dream which continues to haunt his true disciples. That is the explanation of the affinities between surrealism and Marxism—but of their contradictions as well. For they are two divergent roads. Surrealism is much more akin to anarchism or to trotskyism, towards which Breton was to lean. Aragon was not to succeed in becoming the party's official poet save through agreeing to renounce surrealism for neo-realism and through allowing the intense concentration of poetic activity as conceived by Rimbaud to be diluted in a facile rhetoric.

This performance, of course, has ever since been felt to be a betrayal of poetry. Poetry is degraded when it becomes no more than an instrument. Then prose, said Valéry, has the greater excellence. When one has tasted the magic philter, every other conception of poetry seems flat. Rimbaud provoked a crisis that is with us yet. True, we did have Valéry after Mallarmé. With him, poetry became once again an exploration of the possibilities of language. He caught, in incomparable alliterations, the purest music of the language. What was inadvertent in Racine or in Lamartine:

> *La colombe au col noir roucoule sur les toits*

became in his case a conscious and canny art.

> *Dormeuse amas doré d'ombres et d'abandons.*

But Valéry made no disciples. Or, if he made any, who knows them? He was the pure academician. He resumed, in the spirit of a Malherbe, the guardianship of the language. His verses remain in the memory as those particles of radium of which Thibaudet spoke and which have a quickening power. But this vocation as academician, as manager of the department of literature—what relish would this hold for someone who had caught from Rimbaud the corrupt gaminess of the poetic act? Poetry after Rimbaud could lead only to Bicêtre, to the Santé, or to Chartreuse. It could thenceforth make only monks, madmen, or felons—Artaud, Reverdy, or Genêt.

Poetic activity after Rimbaud became a serious and dangerous activity, engaging the whole man. And 'for that reason one hesitates to denounce it out of hand. For is this not to appeal again to poetry as springing from the sacred mountain? Is this not to rob it of its wild gaminess? Is this not to come back to a poetic discourse that only lends significance to the message which is the pretext for it, and to which it only adds ornamentation? Is this not to return to poetry as prettification—to a poetic decor? Or, if poetry is to seek no end but itself, is this not to reduce it to the *bibelot d'inanité sonore* of which Mallarmé spoke, to a stuffy and childish game, to a bloodless parlor diversion?

Still, Rimbaud must be denounced. And the risks involved must be taken. We shall see later where they lead us. It is precisely the great moment of poetic activity as conceived by Rimbaud which we must see our way to rejecting. For in Rimbaud's view poetic activity is genuine only if it is the supreme activity, the one in which man becomes the equal of God, or rather substitutes himself for God. Thierry Maulnier saw this clearly when he wrote:

> Poetry concentrates the mind at the highest point of awareness for a momentary possession of the secrets of the universe. It is not prayer, but creation; and what takes place is not mysticism, but magic.[2]

The objective here is absolute knowledge, where knowledge and power coincide, in an ambition whose Satanic character was clearly perceived by Carrouges.

Rimbaud's was the desperate struggle to return to our lost

[2] Thierry Maulnier, *Introduction à la poésie française*, p. 32.

Paradise, to find anew our glorified bodies, and to be reconciled with the cosmos, without first passing through a conversion of heart. What we are considering here is magical activity literally speaking. Magic here is no simple figure of speech. The first of all temptations was a temptation to magic, an ambition to seize mysterious energies, to steal fire from heaven. Now, this is the temptation of the Promethean poet. Every word of Thierry Maulnier's here is an exact one. We are discussing a "possession of the secrets of the universe," an absolute knowledge, the philosopher's stone. But such knowledge is power. It permits a transmutation of values. It rivals divine creative activity.

But the paradise it sets out to restore is not the Paradise where divine energies create an atmosphere of grace, radiant with charisms. This Paradise only Christ can restore, the tree of life planted in the Paradise of the Church watered by the living water which springs from his pierced heart. The paradise of Rimbaud and of Rilke is the paradise of animal innocence—not Eden before the Fall, but Eden before man, the mysterious threshold where man did not yet exist as separate, not separate from God, but separate from nature. So he was as described by Kierkegaard: "In the state of innocence, man was not an animal, nor was he man, either." This was that ambiguous paradise that had not impinged upon the realm of sin only because it had not impinged upon the realm of conscience, a world of beginnings and of metamorphoses, a limitless night trembling on the sill of light.

Thus the significance attached to poetic activity becomes clear to us. We understand why, from Novalis to Baudelaire, it is haunted by "the bottomless dark." Here we meet the obscure metamorphoses and the new Genesis of the *Chants de Maldoror*; we meet the metallic glare and the inhuman strange-

ness of landscape in St-John Perse; we meet the efforts of
Michaux to find the ultimate primitive. All surrealism, is it not,
is an effort to liberate imaginative creation from the control of
ethics, to regain the autonomy of a pre-human world?

Poetry thus considered is the religion of primordial night,
of the *"sainte de l'abîme"* which Nerval spoke of, abolishing
time and thus being both "the first and the last." Through
poetic activity, the poet is ingulfed in

> *ce puits sombre*
> *Seuil de l'ancien chaos dont le néant est l'ombre*
> *Spirale engloutissant les mondes et les jours.*

The poetic act is a spiritual exercise, but a spiritual exercise of
a mysticism of darkness, whose night is not the overwhelming
brightness of divine light which blinded the sight of John of
the Cross, but the "vast, black, and bottomless" night which is
the negative radiance of primordial nothing. Mysticism perhaps, but an inverted mysticism, whose itinerary Rolland de
Renéville described in *Le sens de la nuit*.

To sum up: The business of poetry for the past century has
been to constitute itself as a mystical experience, belonging to
a mysticism in which poetic activity is presented as an absolute
experience. True, this has conferred upon it a seriousness, a
dark luminousness, a dignity that it never knew when it was
but a handmaid. The handmaid wished herself queen. But
this sacrilegious ambition is precisely what we are denouncing.
We are denouncing it because this mysticism is a false mysticism, which has nothing in common with that of John of the
Cross, but is the topsy-turvy image of it. We denounce it also
as a mystification—a hoax, because it betrays itself as feckless
and ultimately a joke. It is a brief flash, which then leaves man

the prey of the darkness. It is a perversion of poetic activity itself, a distortion of its genuine significance. And that is why it has brought about the crisis of poetry.

Thus, poetic activity does not represent man's highest activity. His highest activity is the mystical, which has to do with a different realm, and is an obscure grasp, in naked faith, of the Trinity as dwelling in what Tauler called the deeps of the soul, where it effects man's sanctification and divinization. Mystical activity is thus incommensurable with poetic activity. And it is an abuse of the word *mysticism* to apply it to poetry. Thierry Maulnier was right on this point. Henri Bremond created many a confusion in this whole matter by likening the poetical trance to mystical recollection. Even if he did point out the differences, it was still going too far when he instituted a comparison between two radically different departures which have nothing in common but certain analogous psychological phenomena. Poetry is not prayer.

Accordingly, poetical activity from the Christian point of view must be relegated to a second place. It belongs to the realm of mind, and not to the realm of charity. But will it not then lose all its value? Will the poet not then become a mere rimesmith? Will the loftiness that the nineteenth century found in it not be brought to nought? We say the very opposite. One of the great errors of our time is refusing to see an activity as valuable unless it is raised to the absolute, whether it be poetic activity, scientific invention, or revolutionary activity. It is precisely in this pretension that lies what we have been calling mystification. It is the business of Christianity to challenge this pretension and to assert that there is no mysticism save that of God. All human activities are by nature relative. Claudel sensed this aright; for him, poetic activity was indeed something consequential, but its product instinct with an irony that punctures, not true greatness, but Satanic pretense. Thus he attested the nugatory character of what Rimbaud set afoot.

But for all that, poetic activity—within its own realm—is not cheapened, but rated at its true value. And the question that confronts us now is this one (and it seems to me the essential question) : Granted poetic activity is infinitely inferior to mystical activity, still, is it bereft of all value in the realm of the sacred? Is the choice we have to make the choice between a sacral, but sacrilegious activity, and a profane—and de-sacralized—activity? Will not poetic activity renounce false gods only at the price of renouncing any God? In the liturgy of the Blessed Sacrament, did not Dante, while leaving the first place to Francis and Dominic, nevertheless slip into hiding among the angelic musicians? Did not Dante, in fact, present Virgil as guide through the first stages of the mystical journey, until Virgil's place was taken by Beatrice and Bernard? After having denounced a false conception of the relationship be-tween mysticism and poetry, we ought to represent the true state of affairs.

For that, we must come back to the nature of poetic activity. True, one may speak of a poetic state of grace which is a sudden perception of a harmony resolving all the dissonances. And true, there is such a thing as poetic inspiration, not in the sense of a visitation of the divine *Pneuma*, disclosing the spiritual significance of things, but in the sense of a sudden revelation of a hitherto hidden correspondence among the cosmic realities. And true, too, the poet experiences, in the presence of this revelation, the feeling of something being com-municated to him. Du Bos once admirably defined the spiritual: "The sense of a plus where we had been unaware of a minus," that is, pure gain—total gratuity. And, true enough, in the presence of this gratuitous communication, the poet feels suffused with a sort of gratitude. One may even, if one wishes, in this sense speak of poetry as a spiritual exercise.

But Du Bos, with deep insight, distinguished among the various grades of what he called "the spiritual in the realm of literature." First, there is that of Shelley, wherein the poetic imagination is dissolved and diffused in a sort of communion with the cosmos. Such were those subtle fluids from which Maurice de Guérin could never emerge, and over which Rilke had to triumph in an heroic effort to exist in his difference. On the next higher level the spiritual designates, in Du Bos' scheme, "human activity wherein is elucidated the activity of genius," where the fragments of images, caught into the orbit of the nucleus of the person (whose glorified body, so to speak, they constitute) become significative of the life of the mind and give pure idea a visible face.

Poetic activity is always perception of correspondences. Here, we return to Baudelaire. It is precisely the intuitive grasp of symbolic relationships between heterogeneous areas. This can take place on the level of sensation.

Les parfums, les couleurs et les sons se répondent.

And it is the cosmic spiritual. But these correspondences may obtain between images and the psyche, between the macrocosm and the microcosm. The world appears to man as the mirror in which his own image is reflected:

... san vous, belles fontaines,
Ma beauté, ma douleur, me seraient incertaines.

Here we come into the realm of myth, which is the royal domain of poetry.

But further on comes still another stage. If the cosmos is a mirror in which man contemplates his own image, it is also the reflection of another Face. Mircea Eliade has shown how the various constituents of the cosmos—the moon and the waters, rock and tree, woman and serpent—are hierophanies, revelations of mystery, which waken the sense of the sacred in the soul. And it is on this level that beauty becomes insupportable, that is, when it becomes indeed Beauty, when the weight of an angel weighs upon the heart, for "the beautiful is nothing but the beginning of the terrible; scarcely do we sustain it," said Rilke. The angel, then, pierces the spirit with his sharp arrow and opens the wellspring of adoration in the heart.

Therefore, there does exist a point where poetry and the sacred meet. And this is the point where poetic experience and (to use Maritain's expression) natural mystical experience meet. This is a certain apprehension of God through his manifestation in the visible world. It is this particular significance of poetic activity that Claudel, being awakened to the dignity of poetic activity by Mallarmé and Rimbaud and freed from their "black demons," rediscovered. The catastrophe of *Igitur* is answered by the *Te Igitur* of his *Messe là-bas*, through which alone "the purified heart" understands "the odor of the rose":

> We know that the world is, in effect, a text, and that it speaks to us, humbly and joyously, of its own emptiness, but also of the presence of someone else, namely, its Creator.[3]

But this apprehension of mystery under the appearance of images through the intermediary of conversion of heart, if it appears as the goal and summit of poetic activity, is only the first step of the stairway of mysticism.

[3] Paul Claudel, *Positions et Propositions*, I, 206.

This, then, is our conclusion: Poetry has attained, in our times, to an awareness of its specific direction such as it never attained to in the past. Oh, this specific direction itself did exist, previously, in the real poets—in Scève and in Donne, in Racine and in Dante; but there never was this full awareness of poetry's specific nature. Yet poetry reached this awakening to full self-awareness only through a kind of original sin, when, a victim of its own dizzying loftiness, it thought it could not *be* save by determining to be *all*. Thus it became a captive of the dark angels and the butt of their derision. But perhaps upon emerging from this tragic adventure, on the difficult roads along which it now toils, it is in the process of discovering, in humility, its true dignity.

CHAPTER V

What Is
Your Vision
of
the World?

IT IS the very way the question is framed that nettles me. Am I to explain dutifully how I see the world? Then others will explain likewise their ways of seeing it. The collection of views will be presented. And the public will compare and choose. All this has little interest for me. For accepting this challenge already constitutes a choice. It is the choice of singularity as against truth. What I think is not important. The important thing is to know what is. And if I cannot tell what is, it is better for me to be silent. But is asserting that what one says is truth not pretentiousness, an insult to others, and intolerable self-conceit? It would be so if speaking of truth were a way of justifying and reassuring one's self. But to speak truth is to convict both one's self and others at the same time. And it is even the only way to bring any and every self-justification into court.

The first question is one of method. Now, the essential principle of method is distinction of realms. Pascal, because he had the outlook of geometry, knew that the spirit of geometry is incommensurable with the realities of the human person. "A single thought of a man is worth more than all the universe," said St. John of the Cross. Making man a part of nature is the first error—and also reducing human history to a part of natural history. When everything has been explained, there is left over what Jankelevich called the "I know not what" and the "almost nothing," the indefinable something which is precisely everything. And the error lies in failing to recognize that this "almost nothing" is "everything."

Primitive experience is essentially global. But it is the very business of the mind to distinguish among the various levels, the various planes of existence, each irreducible to any other. The complete man is one who expresses himself on all the levels. "Christianity," said Jacques Rivière, "is that which allows the maximum of feelings at every instant." The universe of scientism is one which imprisons itself in the world of geometry. It is the universe of marxism. It is the world of ennui, of repetition. Simone de Beauvoir rightly depicted it under this aspect in *Tous les hommes sont mortels*. It is characterized by a feeling of captivity, of being stifled. But there exists also a prison of spiritualism.

The only universe where I can really breathe is the one where I can pass from one level to another. It is the universe of correspondences. When the lightning cracks, the old peasant woman makes the sign of the cross; the village schoolteacher laughs at her. Is lightning anything but the discharge of atmospheric electricity? It is the old woman who is right; and it is not she who is being silly. Here I am one with Guénon in his contempt for positivism. The lightning storm has also a sacral dimension. It is a hierophany, Eliade was to say. That it is, as well. It exists on several planes of existence. And intelligence consists in understanding this. Baudelaire detected a certain mediocrity of mind in ineptitude at grasping the sacral dimension of the cosmos. But Guénon was wrong in rejecting the criticism of the scientific mind. For it is by the test of that criticism that the substantiality of the sacred is made plain.

I approve minds applied to, and submitted to, the real, able to be instructed by it. And I willingly take Bergson's tack when he distinguishes between the realm of matter and the realm of memory. It is the business of the intelligence to distinguish. Nothing is more frightful than what Rivière called "*manque de crête*," indifference such as no longer perceives the various realms in their heterogeneity. I understand Max Scheler when he shows that personal love cannot be explained in terms of sexual love or of crowd psychology. And I read twice when Du Bos' pages distinguish among Shelley's cosmic spiritual in which personal life dissolves, Wordsworth's personal spiritual, which supposes access to responsibility, and Bérulle's divine spiritual, which is divine inspiration.

The danger always lies in reduction which is an impoverishment. The honest thing is to acknowledge things that are irreducible. That is why I distrust dialectic. Or rather, I protest against its abuse. There can be dialectic within a given realm: Thus liberty and community are the two poles of every economic dialectic, and are always relative to each other. But dialectic never enables us to pass from one realm to another. There is no dialectic of spirit and matter, time and eternity, good and evil. There is contrariety or contradiction.

Similarly, I am opposed to every thoroughgoing evolutionism, whether biological or technological. The idea that the maturation of matter can end up in the birth of spirit, or that technological progress can modify man morally, has always seemed to me the prime example of a lack of discernment. It is true that there is a biosphere, a noosphere, and a Christosphere. They correspond to the three realms of Pascal. But, and this is the point, it must be insisted with Pascal that there is no passing from one to another of these, which are irreducible universes through which an integral experience is extended. It is a childish notion to suppose that the movement of time brings us towards eternity. Eternity is the passage to a different plane.

Just as there is a prison of matter, so there is a prison of spirit, inclosing man within himself. Spirit is a highly equivocal word. It defines a level of being—that of liberty and of thought. Yet this is but one level. Spiritualism fixes itself upon this level and incloses itself there. It is just as much closed, in this sense, as materialism. It presumes to bring everything under its jurisdiction. The spirit of man thus becomes the measure of being. It constitutes the highest plane of being. Such is the idea of the various humanisms and personalisms. Respect for others becomes the sole norm of conduct. Individual or collective, this humanism refers man only to himself, and absorbs him in the contemplation of his own greatness. It is correct in acknowledging the transcendence of spirit as regards nature; but it limits itself to this level.

Here again we must return to Pascal. All spirits taken together do not equal one act of charity. And for Pascal, as a good Augustinian, the realm of charity is that of divine love and the supernatural life. This realm can be called spiritual, but spiritual then refers, not to the life of the spirit, but to the life of the Holy Spirit. It is not the spirit's becoming aware of its immanence to itself, but of the divine power which raises it above itself. After traversing the world of bodies and the starry sky, Idythius penetrates first into the interior universe, into the sphere of the spirit, and circles upon the celestial vault; but he does not stop there; he launches beyond himself, discovering, more interior to himself than himself, the primordial source from which at every instant his personal existence springs.

Adoration is a dimension of every integral humanism. It is always a falling short to be powerless to open one's self to the special realm of greatness which is constituted of divine splendors. For biblical humanism, man is at once king of the universe and the subject of God. Six days are given him in which to subdue nature to himself by his labors. But the seventh is the day on which, by adoration, he recognizes God's sovereignty over him. A world without prayer is not simply an irreligious world, it is an inhuman world. The true city, says La Pira, is "the one where men have their houses and where God has his house." A world which is only a world of work, and not a world of liturgy, is a world where one cannot breathe. Prayer is a struggle to save man from asphyxiation.

Exactness of thought requires the acknowledgment of the various levels even when the thinker has not reached them all. Giving testimony to the truth consists in judging one's self, and not in justifying one's self. It may be that I cannot fulfil myself on each of the levels. But it is one thing to be blind, and another to deny the existence of the light. And that is why it is possible to be at once sincere and true. "I have jumped man," Rilke had the courage to say, in his vertiginous passage from animal to angel. But that was not denying man. I do not know God, the thinker has the right to say. But this does not mean: There is no God. And perhaps this is precisely what intelligence consists in—not being imprisoned in experience, but being able to judge experience in the name of truth.

It must be clear that we are concerned here, not with what will sit most comfortably, but with rigor of method. Similarly, acknowledgment of a transcendent order is the very opposite of an easy way out. It constitutes a most terrible menace to my desire to be my own man, and to be self-sufficient. It brings into my life love and love's huge unsettlingness. It is no security against adventure, but acceptance of adventure. And that is why I dread it. The most clearsighted recognize this. They call for respite in order to fulfil themselves. The weight of divine glory seems to them too heavy to bear. They jealously defend a world cut to their measure, a human world, as against a world divine, of outrageous measure, and inhuman.

So should I like to shut myself up in my own realm, and to have none but tasks suited to me and apt to give me satisfaction. But it does not depend on me to be thrown into this abyss where eternity does not permit me even to recognize myself and where I must learn at last that it is in deprivation that riches consist. A world tailored to me would be more reassuring. I should feel myself more at home there. I am loath to go outside my familiar horizon. Now, God is precisely what will never be familiar to me, and will never cease to be a source of astonishment to me, and of holy dread. That is, at least, if we are speaking of the real God—not of one who is only the projection of my frustrated desires, but of one whose irruption tumbles down the flimsy constructions in which I thought to take refuge.

Here a new aspect of the question comes into view. Up to this point, reality was exhibiting its various levels before my eyes. All that was required of me was to be attentive. I grasped its various levels both in their irreducibleness and in their mutual correspondences. For if they constituted heterogeneous realms, still they displayed a whole collection of interconnections, which make up the universe of analogy. The world is in the image of God. Thus passage between the two is possible; and the universe of contemplation consists in this marvelous aptitude the mind has to move in a world of multiple dimensions without being imprisoned in any of them, nor even in itself. God in this sense is freedom.

But in this universe, I am not simply a spectator. I know it so well only because I am involved in it. It is not only symbolic, but dramatic. God is not simply the supreme realm in the hierarchy of essences; he is also the totality of being, the existence on which all existence is basically dependent. And here comes the fundamental difficulty. If God exists, how can anything exist outside God, since the fulness of existence is exhausted once and for all in him? What interest does existence hold for me if all I can do is repeat, in some worse way, what has once and for all been accomplished perfectly? Does not God's existence thus cancel out my existence?

It is certainly true that God's existence throws any claim of mine out of court. Yet for all that it does not destroy my existence, but only stops my appropriation of my existence. It enjoins me to acknowledge it as received, from each instant to the next. "What powers do you have, that did not come to you by gift? And if they came to you by gift, why do you boast of them, as if there were no gift in question?" [1 Cor. 4:7] There exactly is the condition of created being. It implies a radical dependence. I do not exist save as I am (like a word) being uttered by another. And ratifying my existence means recognizing this dependence. But this comes in conflict with my passion to belong to myself. The clearsighted man grasps this very well. He knows that what is, always is "by gift." That is why he takes refuge in non-acceptance. "This at least is mine, all mine," said Rivière of his sins.

But this declaration of my dependence should be for me the most exalting of discoveries. It means in effect that I do not exist save as I am loved. It radically destroys my solitude. To exist means my being already in connection with another. And ratifying my existence means recognizing this relationship; and responding to this gift by giving thanks means having found my way to communication. Nor is any inferiority implied by this relationship, which corresponds, instead, to the very structure of being. The Christian dogma of the Trinity expresses, in effect, this paradoxical reality: that *three* is as primordial as *one,* which is to say that love is coeternal with existence and plays its part in the structure of being, at the utter bottom of things. And hence this relative character of mine is nothing but the created epiphany of the uncreated mystery.

With this, I came to the second fundamental certainty. The first was the distinction of realms. The second is the evidential quality of love. I might doubt, strictly, the exterior world. It is, in a sense, interior to me, and might be only the projection of my mind. But I cannot doubt the reality of another than myself. It is love which brings me in touch with the undoubtable, that is, with what resists me, with what I do not have at my disposition, with what I cannot refuse the right to exist apart from me, and with what I am forced to acknowledge the value of. "Every license, save against love," said Barrès. And love is in fact the only thing by virtue of which I cannot refuse to be limited without renouncing my own self.

Now, what is true of this other is eminently true of God. God is signally the one who resists me. It is indeed by virtue of that fact that he forces himself upon me. For if I had invented him, I should have made him more accommodating. But I recognize that it is for this very reason that he disturbs me, that he upsets my settled notions and my disposition to run my life as I please. I am faced with this paradox. It is precisely because I do not want him to exist that I am forced to recognize that he does exist. I am far too interested in having him not exist for me not to view with suspicion my wish that this were the situation. I first learn to acknowledge him through my vain attempts to bend him to my wishes; he will subsequently teach me to love him by trying to bend my wishes to his.

Thus the world of existence reveals itself to us as a universe of persons united by love. Theological ontology is an ontology of love. Love exists eternally in God in the Trinity of the divine Persons. The community of spiritual persons united by love is an epiphany of the divinity which is Trinity. And between the divine Trinity and the human community there exists a bond of love and of communication which is the Person of Christ, true God and true man, "in whom God has reconciled all things among themselves and with himself," and who is thus mediator of all things, the cosmic tree reuniting what is below and what is on high, what is East and what is West, by the outreaching sign of his cross.

And this brings us to the third indubitable truth, which is history. History is the junction-point of symbol and drama, the perspective in which all things assume meaning. It is by nature a disclosure, for it bears not upon necessities but upon facts, because it is the domain of grace. It alone is mystery properly speaking for St. Paul. For mystery is the hidden secret of the destiny of mankind and of the cosmos. And only the immolated Lamb of the Apocalypse opens the book sealed with the seven seals and containing it: "The gods have buried the secret of the descent of things somewhere, but where then have they hidden the stone which covers it, o Melibeus?" It is to this question in the *Centaure* that the Lamb supplies the answer.

Here again it is Pascal who gives us the rule of method when he shows that what corresponds to the realm of charity is the spirit of prophecy. There are three indubitables: The first is matter, to which the spirit of geometry corresponds; the second is the person, to which corresponds the spirit of shrewdness;

the third is Jesus Christ, and here there corresponds the spirit of prophecy. Each of these realms envelops the preceding one. Spirit envelops matter, but Jesus Christ in turn envelops spirit. He is himself the Logos, divine Reason and Power, "through whom all things were made," who irrupts into time to repossess the creation which belongs to him in order to bring it to maturity, give it its ultimate meaning, fit it into an intelligible history. Jesus Christ is the Truth in the realest sense, that is, it is he in whom is revealed the ultimate and hidden sense of everything.

History here indicates first of all that there are divine works —*mirabilia*. The Bible is this history of the works of God, which are of another order than the works of men, their great inventions, their masterpieces. But the works of God are greater and of another order, which is the order of charity, to which I am introduced by the spirit of prophecy, which is understanding of sacred history in the light of the Holy Spirit, who is the author of that history. "Jesus Christ made no great inventions. But he was holy, holy, holy. Holy to God, terrible to the devil." There is an order of greatness which is that of the greatnesses of Jesus Christ. And Pascal, who knew the greatnesses of geometry and the greatnesses of thought, knew that those of Jesus Christ surpassed them infinitely. The right mind is one which recognizes each order of greatness for what it is.

History next means eschatology, that is, tension towards the last outcome of all. It is this that basically differentiates the mythical vision and the biblical vision. In the mythical vision, the essential event existed as an archetype in primordial time. And concrete time is never anything but degradation, forever combated by rite. In contrast, for the Bible the essential event is looked for in the future. "No longer remember the things that are past. Behold, I shall work a new wonder." Creation is a prospect. That is to say that the brightness of the first creation will be lost in the brightness of the new creation. History proceeds from glory to glory. At the end of his long wanderings, Odysseus, the man of the cosmic religion, returns to the place from which he started. In Greek, the *Odyssey* is called *nostoi,* meaning turnings home. Odysseus is the man of nostalgia, who is in quest of the irremediably lost time of the paradise of childhood. In contrast, Abraham, the man of historical religion, left Ur and its familiar scenes forever, to go forward in pure faith towards the unknown land which God would show him.

History indicates in the third place that the eschatological event is already with us. This is what Cullmann has shown in his book on Christ and time. This fact condemns exclusive faith in progress, just as eschatology condemns exclusive faith in tradition. And here is the greatest paradox of the faith. It consists in asserting that just as nothing in the past had been of so great importance as Jesus Christ, so no discovery or invention, no revolution will ever bring us anything as important as Jesus Christ. Jesus Christ is therefore the last end, that beyond which there is nothing—that is, he in whom salvation is already given. This does not mean that after him there is no time, but that time which follows him is in some sense interior to him and is constituted by the extension of his dimensions, until the Church, which is his body, has attained its fulness.

Thus history is not the homogeneous movement, whether cyclic or evolutive, of natural history. It is differentiated into heterogeneous epochs, of which Jesus Christ constitutes the central point of articulation. And this is true, not only of human history, but also of cosmic history, embracing all reality. The earth is not the physical center of the universe, as medieval science believed; nor is it necessarily the center of complexity, the central axis of evolution, as Teilhard de Chardin believed; but it is the theological center, inasmuch as it is the place wherein was accomplished the decisive event for all creation, material or spiritual, past, present, or future. "In him all things have their subsistence," said Paul.

It is still true that between these heterogeneous epochs there are correspondences—the analogy of the divine operations with the various moments of the history of salvation. Thus the coming forth from Egypt, the resurrection of Christ, baptism, and the resurrection on the last day are all analogous operations of deliverance. Here there arises a new symbolism, which is this relation of the successive moments of the history of salvation. The knowledge of these correspondences is the content of prophecy. And since the history of salvation subsumes all history, it also embraces natural history and human history. Thus the various realms, or orders, which we have distinguished not only indicate different densenesses of existence, but spread before us like the stages of total history.

The drama we have spoken of takes on, in turn, an historical dimension. It is not only the timeless confrontation of God and man. It is the conflict between two histories; one consisting of the unfolding of God's designs; the other, of the unfolding of men's designs. This conflict of the two histories St. Augustine described in his *City of God*. This, too, is a history cosmic in nature. It is the conflict between Christ and the forces of evil. For this reason the mystery of Christ is the mystery not only of the incarnation of the Word, but of his crucifixion as well. It reached its climax when the Word descended into hell, that is, into the abyss of evil inaccessible to man's good will, in order to destroy evil in its poisonous root and to open for mankind—on the day of the resurrection—transfigured existence.

* * *

In the presence of death, all speech is superficial. It is a mere

noise of words, with which we try to distract or perhaps re-
assure ourselves. But silence is better. Only one thing merits
utterance in the face of death, and that is an acknowledgment
of the resurrection of the dead. "In short," wrote Brice Parain,
"there are really only two solutions: strict anonymity or the
resurrection of the flesh in glory." But this is a hard word, and
who can listen to it? It convicts me in my reasoning and
judges me in my actions. But that is why I can utter it,
because it is not my word, but the Word. I have listened to it
and I have believed it. And because I have believed it, I must
speak it in my turn. It is a scandal for the Jew in me, it is
folly for the Greek in me. But it is precisely because it is
neither the word of the Jew nor the word of the Greek that
it is the Word of God and that it is truth.

CHAPTER VI

Foundations of the Faith

OUR RESPONSIBILITY to assert our faith in the presence of the men of our time is a singular one. For what we assert is really something improbable; and it is normal for us to come up at first against an attitude of incredulity. What I mean by that is that the assertions required of us by our faith, namely, that the destiny which is ours goes beyond the frontiers of this life, since we are called by God to an eternal destiny; that the essential event of human history has already taken place; that never will any revolution or any amount of scientific progress bring us anything so important as the resurrection of Jesus Christ—these are affirmations of singular audacity.

They therefore confront us with a heavy intellectual responsibility. These assertions—have we the right to make them? Have we the right to involve the full responsibility of our liberties with them? Is the question here one simply of our preaching a view of the world which seems congenial to us; or, instead, do we really have the right, and the duty, to declare to every man, no matter who he is, that he will one day be judged by Jesus Christ, and that this trial is the only one of ultimate importance in any and every human life? Have we the right and duty to say to some marxist associate of ours:

"Because I really love you, I am obliged to tell you that one day you are going to be judged by Jesus Christ." For this is what we mean by "believing." That is to say that Christianity is not one philosophy side by side with a number of other philosophies, but the ultimate truth about man's destiny. Well, does Christianity really mean that for us? And doesn't the feebleness of our testimony come from our perhaps not having faith?

So, before thinking of giving the faith to others, we have to examine ourselves to determine whether we have it ourselves. Now one sure thing is that the way most of us conduct ourselves gives others the impression that we do not have faith. For, watching us, they say to themselves: "If it were really true what they say, then it ought to show up in their lives in some much more striking way." And often, in fact, we give unbelievers the impression that we are attached to Christianity, of course, as a way of looking at life that happens to suit us best, but not that it is *the* truth, period, that is, the only sense there is to man's life, a meaning that is God's plan and that every man must face up to. This is not a question of dogmatism; it is not a question of our wishing to impose our views on other people. In fact, it is not a question of our views at all. The faith is not something I adhere to because it is a world view that pleases me. We do not pick out our faith as we pick out a hat. I was recently talking with a young woman who said to me: "My husband tells me that by nature he is more Protestant than anything." The problem is not to determine whether Protestantism suits me best, or whether Buddhism suits me best, or whether Catholicism suits me best. One is not a Protestant because he has a taste for a certain liberty; one is not a Catholic because of whatever imaginable connivance with authority. One is a Catholic because he thinks Catholicism is true. And whether that suits me or upsets me, pleases me or

displeases me, puts me at ease or makes me ill at ease, I am
obliged to profess it—as true for myself and for other people.

Thus all this is a serious matter. Speaking of the faith is a
grave responsibility. It is a responsibility which we assume in
the presence of other people. We must therefore determine
what this means. What I should like to do is just to examine
myself to see what the faith means, what its nature is, and what
its claims are. Have I really the right to believe all these things,
in all intellectual honesty? Have I the right to stake my intelligence on the word of Jesus Christ? Have I the right to assert
that it is the final answer to man's fate, to the riddles which
it poses?

The first thing to be done is to determine what realm faith
is in. There is in most men a religious sense. Atheism is a
modern phenomenon in the first place, and, in the second place,
a phenomenon ultimately less widespread than people think.
Recently I heard the pastor of a large Paris parish tell me that
the more contact he had with working-class circles the more he
noticed how ready they were to receive the Christian message;
and he added: "More, alas, than in middle-class circles." It is
sure that there is in every human soul an openness to the sacred,
to mystery, to the world beyond, and that what in Jaspers'
language are called "limit situations"—confrontation of suffering, love, death, liberty—put man in the presence of realities
which he is quite well aware transcend him. And, from this
point of view, it may be said that the religious sense is a part
of human nature. I myself think that its disappearance constitutes a maiming of human nature, and that a man in whom
there is not openness to God is a man mutilated in an essential
part of himself.

Of this quest for God it may be said that "religions" are

the expression. And, in this sense, all religions have their truth, and we must give them their due as representing what I shall call man's quest for God. Men have always sought for God. And each religion is the way in which men of one age or of one land have given this quest life. We have only to read some of the religious books of India (I am thinking of the Bhagavadgîtâ), certain poems by the great Moslem mystics (I am thinking of Al-Hallaj, whose wonderful mystical poems Louis Massignon has published), we have only to be in contact with the African world to grasp what a wealth of deep religious values are to be found in all the civilizations of the world. This constitutes what I shall call the "religious world," which is not yet the world of the faith. One may wonder whether, in our time, the crisis within this religious world is not like an obstacle preliminary to the wakening of faith. But what concerns me for what I am trying to define here is that we are not yet at this moment in the actual realm of faith. It is not necessary to be Christian in order to believe there is a God. All human civilizations have this religious aspect. It may be said that religions are part of the patrimony of the human race and represent one of its essential riches.

In the domain of faith we reach quite another order. Belief does not mean believing there is a God; it means believing that God intervenes in human life. The object of faith is an event, or a series of events. Belief means, in effect, believing that God spoke to Abraham, freed the people from Egypt, became flesh in the womb of Mary, raised up from among the dead the humanity to which he was united, and is present in the midst of us in the Holy Eucharist. And that is the supreme paradox. For men in fact do allow that we acknowledge, in a higher world, a divinity which surpasses us. But that God intervenes in the course of human life, and that in the midst of us there are divine operations going on—this seems absolutely scandalous. This latter in fact is what the greater part of men reject. They reject the supernatural.

Now that is exactly what the faith asserts. The sacred book of Christians is not some or other treatise of religious philosophy, it is a history—Sacred History. To believe means to accept the Bible, the Old and the New Testament. Now, what the Old and New Testaments contain is history. But there are two histories. There is the history of the great things men have done since the beginning, the history of the great cultures, the history of science, the history of discoveries and inventions, and political history; and this history is real history; it is the story of the great works of man; and it gives glory to man. We, however, we believe that there is another history, more profound. That is to say, there are things which are not man's work, but God's, and these works of God are infinitely greater than the greatest works of man. They surpass, that is, as Pascal put it, the works of man in proportion as the order of charity surpasses the order of intelligence and the order of physical bodies. To be a Christian, then, is to believe that there are divine operations in our midst, and that these divine operations are what constitute the greatest thing in the world. To be a Christian is to believe that a Thérèse of Lisieux in her Carmelite convent is more important in the hierarchy of values than the greatest of political figures or the greatest of scientists. For her importance is of another, and greater, order.

And to be a Christian is to believe that these divine operations are not merely past events, but that we are living in the full tide of sacred history, that we are living in a world in which God continues to act, and that, as the Protestant exegete Cullmann has so beautifully put it, the sacraments are the continuation into the time of the Church of the great works of

God in the Old and in the New Testament. This is the magnificent proclamation which it is ours to make. This one thing we have to say to the marxists, to the atheistic humanists, namely, that they miss perceiving the most profound dimension of human existence, which is the one which God brings about in man; ultimately, then, we reproach them with being superficial—with reaching, that is, only the surface of man, and failing to plumb the abysses of existence.

The more I study marxism, what strikes me most is this same shockingly superficial quality. There may be found in it some things that have validity on the level of the world of appearances, on the level of the dialectic of economic life for example; but it leaves untouched what constitutes man's most essential side. And this is why we are so keenly aware, in rejecting marxism, that what we are defending is not only God, but man. It is man in the fulness of his dimension, in his threefold relationship, that is, to the world, to other people, and to God. And that is why we shall never desist from our assertion of the divine dimension of human existence, because it seems to us a constituent of the only integral humanism, the only one that gives full justice to the dignity of human nature.

But let us turn directly to the substance of the act of faith. To believe means to believe that the Word of God was made flesh in the womb of Mary. You see the insolence of such an assertion. In the presence of a marxist, of an atheist, of a scientist, we know what it will provoke. We can imagine what they will begin to say. If we do not dare to take the responsibility for our faith in all its paradoxicalness, if we let it be understood that it might be only a more or less mythological representation of some or other subjective phenomenon, then we have already begun to lighten the ship, and from that moment on have charted a career of betrayals. To be a

Christian, in contrast, means insisting that nothing more nor less than this divine irruption into human life is exactly the joyous news, the magnificent, the splendid message that we proclaim. But being a Christian also means being capable of justifying this assertion in our own eyes and in other people's eyes, and our claim to the right to make it.

Regarding the object of faith I should like to make the final point that, since it bears on a divine event, it can only be one and universal. It is not the expression of the religious sensibility of one people or of one race. There is no worse betrayal of the Gospel than to be willing to make it out to be the religion of the West. Christianity is not one certain vision of the world. It is not a system which we accept because it suits us. The one and only problem is to determine whether something did happen. There is no other question. Did Christ rise from the dead or not? If so, this is of absolute interest for any and every man. We are not talking about a symbolization or projection, but about a real event. The question, then, is determining whether this event is real. If I am not persuaded that it is so, then I do not have the faith. I may have a Christian sensibility, I may be desirous that the spiritual values which are those of the Gospel will remain those of the free world, and that civilization will be inspired by the liberal principles I call the Christian mystique rather than by the socialist doctrine of the "people's democracies." But from that moment on, what I am defending is not the faith, it is some liberty or other, which does not come very high anyhow, of whose lesser worth I am aware, and which, like many of my contemporaries, I take advantage of while I have it, but with the vague feeling that it is not worth a whole lot of bother to defend.

We think we have the right to express the affirmations of

our faith; we have the right to express them to everyone; and in particular we have the right to tell them to our atheist associates; and, if we have the right, we have necessarily the duty to do so. For if we express it, it is not as a personal opinion, such as we might hesitate to force on other people, but as a fact, one that forces itself upon us, whether it is agreeable to us or disagreeable, whether it follows the line of our own thinking or runs counter to it, whether we find consolation in it or, instead, it is something that balks our determination to run our lives as we please. For me, one of the least satisfactory proofs for the existence of God is the following: "I have a desire for happiness. But no earthly object can fully satisfy this desire. Therefore, God exists." Were I an unbeliever, this reasoning would immediately arouse my suspicions. I should already have a deep-seated impression that God is only the projection into infinity of a certain emotional need of mine and that it was I who was fashioning him in my own image. No, I experience the fact that he exists because I run up against him and because, if ever it were I that had fashioned him, I should certainly have made quite a different job of it. As it is, I am obliged to accommodate myself to him. I am obliged to take him just as he is. No, I never made him, in my image. I am the one who finally has to come down to doing things his way. And there's the rub that makes me know I am in contact with the real: when I feel, that is, something which resists me, that I have no control of, and that, on the contrary, I must finally end up by adapting myself to, making way, giving up, against my will, and while dragging my feet. But there is no way out. This is the way it is, and I have to put up with it. Thus am I aware, in sober fact, that I am in the presence of something real, and no creation of my imagination or of my sensibility.

But for all that, it remains true that affirmation of the faith is an extravagant assertion all the same. The assertion—in 1962—of the resurrection of the body; the assertion—in 1962 —of the incarnation of the Word in the womb of Mary—all this is outstanding insolence. Do I have the right, in all intellectual honesty, and with all due rigor of thinking, to make these assertions to everybody? To so-and-so, who is a professor at the university? To so-and-so, the great medical specialist? To so-and-so, the great political figure. To Khrushchev? To Nasser? Well, what my friend La Pira usually does, when he meets some statesman, is to tell him, right off, that God exists, and that the statesman will be judged by Christ. Only then can their conversation begin. The question is ineluctable. The way so many Christians today put their Christianity in their pocket and consider Christ as something optional is a singular delusion. For the question is to determine whether in fact Christ did arise from the dead. If he did, that fact must determine everything else. Christianity is not a matter of private life. If there is anything in the world that is public, that is official, it is Christianity! For it is something that concerns the ultimate destinies of the whole human race and which for that very good reason has to be taken into account by everybody. This is all that I am saying. And this is the weighty interrogation that we are sitting down to. And that is why we must test the solidity of the bases which are the foundations of our faith, so that it will not be, among us, simply the inheritance of a tradition, sentimentally dear to us, or the expression of a certain bent within our own sensibilities, but will be, after having passed through the sieve of a pitiless criticism, something that continues to hold up, so that we may hold to it in the fulness of an adult existence.

Otherwise, there would always exist in us a more or less bad conscience. Faith, for most of us, is something we received from our families, from our circumstances of life. And it is a great grace to have received it in that way. But we reach an age when we have to embrace it in a personal manner, and embrace it as instinct with difficulties and beset by others' claims and questions. It must not fear critical examination. Criticism of this kind has a very great value, so long as it be remembered that its function is not to destroy, not to undermine (as some of our contemporaries think its function to be), but, on the contrary, to test things in order to see whether they stand up. Thus, the business of criticism is to reinforce what is solid and to unsettle what is not; or, if you prefer, looking at the matter in a different way, criticism is useful only when it is the expression of love—when it is not, that is, primarily a desire to destroy, but the will to edify in truth.

Now, there is no escaping the fact that if we take a look at the foundations of our faith, there come at once to mind a host of questions—too many for treatment in this book, but the main ones of which I should like to call to mind, for at this point we reach the essential elements of conscious thought. Among scientists the difficulty is in effect that the intellectual instruments proper to them, of established accuracy in the domains for which they were made, are not utilizable for data in the domain of faith. Whence derives an impression, quite often, of not being on solid ground, of being confronted with a language where meanings are not hard and fast, of being in a field where anybody can say just about anything, since there is no way of determining the truth of anything. As a fellow taxi passenger said to me not very long ago, "It comes to this: Christianity can equally be proved true and be proved not true." The remark is very interesting. If you insist on—this man was a biologist—methods that are proper to physiology, it is plain that you will have no instrument which will allow you to discern, on the level of the data of faith, what is to be retained and to say what is true and what is not true. Whence that feeling on the part of many scientists that in that realm one can say what one likes, and that ultimately—I have heard great scientists say this—you make your choice on purely subjective grounds.

Here is something quite grave, first of all because if one chooses for purely subjective reasons, this means that one waives both justifying one's faith in one's own eyes and justifying it in other people's eyes. For, if it is only my feeling, well, then, I have no right to impose my feeling on other people. That would be intellectual imperialism indeed. I have the right simply to propose what I think. But having faith does not mean that at all. Having faith does not consist in saying: "I believe, for my part, that I think . . . anyhow, I just feel that Christianity is truth . . ." Christ sent me forth into the world, and sent you my readers, whether priests or laymen, not to say, "My feeling is that . . .," but to proclaim the truth, and not my truth or your truth, but truth, period.

Granted, there remains this great difficulty for scientific minds, namely, admitting that there can be evidence as rigorous in the order of testimony as in the order of positive sciences. This, I need not say, reveals a certain lack of any mind for metaphysics, a deficiency which by the way poses a very great problem from the point of view of scientific humanism. The problem of the scientists preoccupies me a great deal these days. I admire them very much. I think that the future belongs to them. But I think that the big thing they are going to need is the balance of a humanistic education such as their university unfortunately does not succeed in giving them and for which, consequently, they must look elsewhere. Here is a very great problem. Scientists are called upon to play a decisive role in the world of tomorrow. It is absolutely indispensable that they be furnished with instruments of thought and expression that are really philosophical, based on methods just as rigorous as the methods of positive sciences, but which require, as scientific methods do, a formal training.

I confess that I am constantly saddened upon seeing, at various conventions, men who are very great scientists or very great technicians, who are strictly logical and exact when speaking about their speciality, but who, as soon as the talk turns to problems of civilization, are satisfied with the most lamentable vaguenesses about "spiritual values"—terms which cover no one has the slightest notion what, and among which reigns the most total confusion. And yet it would seem clearly necessary to know that, when one speaks of "liberty," this can mean five different things at least—and that, in this order, one can have quite as great precision as in the order of scientific problems. There is a rigor of philosophic thought that in its order is absolutely as valid as the rigor of scientific thought.

The problem of testimony arises for men of letters, yet in a different way. The difficulty here is that speech has been so much abused that, finally, one's word is simply no longer taken. The abuse of their word is a characteristic of literary men. A scientist is often someone who has something to say and who is not capable of saying it; a literary man . . . This is grave. Our world is such an intelligent one! When you sit down with your weekly or monthly review (I read the *Express*), you have to marvel at the "refinements," the subtleties of modern-day intelligence—at its astonishing capacity to understand everything and to believe nothing. For that is precisely the definition of an intelligent man, according to one brand of intellectuality today. In this view, the exercise of intelligence is the very purpose of intelligence. And the quality of the language is a more serious matter than any content of the writer's word. To believe in truth reveals in these people's eyes a medieval mentality which is the stamp of only a few old-fashioned minds. This raises very serious questions.

This is the great problem, and it is grave. For it is on a person's word in the very first instance that human relationships rest. For a world where people no longer believe other people's word is a world where any trust becomes out of the question. And it may be wondered whether this spirit of distrust is not poisoning personal relationships among men today. Is there not a kind of doubting-sickness at work at the core of men's souls and destroying even the possibility of communication? And on the level even of our faith do we not harbor a low-grade infection of doubt, such as to make us wonder whether we have ever made an act of theological faith in the full sense of the word, that is, one in which our intelligence is engaged in totally eliminating every reserve, every evasion. I am speaking not of some kind of bet, but of an act totally involving our intelligence with the Word of Christ, without reserving anything to ourselves. And is there not, in this last bit of reserve which we keep so often in connection with faith itself, a certain determination on the part of our intelligence to depend exclusively upon itself, a certain difficulty in giving in, particularly under that pre-eminent form of surrender which is the surrender of the intelligence. This surrender we must never make easily; yet are there not cases where we have the right to make it? Here we reach the rock bottom of the reason why it is so hard for men of today to understand how an act of faith is possible and, even they admit it as possible, to make that act of faith in the full sense of the word. The very idea of being able to speak of absolute truth as based on testimony seems inacceptable.

Now, staying on the human level, without speaking here yet of the testimony of the Gospel directly, we must say that testimony is a way of reaching certitude, a way as valid, in its order, as scientific demonstrations and experiments are in their order. Moreover, this way is the only one which affords access to one certain order of reality. This order of reality is nothing less than the order of persons. Now, if the universe of persons has infinite ascendancy over the order of the natural world, we must declare that the higher we go in the hierarchy of beings, the more does testimony, and not experimentation, become the means of knowledge.

I shall explain these matters further. Experimentation has to do essentially with the order of things which are inferior to man. It bears upon objects. But some one else's person is something of which we can never make an object. We can know another person only to the extent that he chooses to reveal himself to us. And he can reveal himself to us only by giving us his word about himself. This is tantamount to saying that ultimately it is on another's word that we must rely in order to know him. And consequently, on this level, the testimony of some one's word is the sole means of communication among persons. How, then, if God is personal in a pre-eminent degree, and if even on the human level we cannot know the secret of others' persons except to the degree they choose to reveal it to us, how, I say, could we ever know the secret of God otherwise than in the measure in which God chooses to reveal it to us?

Testimony, then, appears as the mode of knowledge which corresponds to higher objects, and furthermore as a means of knowledge which is susceptible, in its own order, of a rigorousness quite equal to that of physical or mathematical demonstrations in their order. This is obvious enough when we turn to historical sciences. No one would dream of questioning the existence of Napoleon or of Julius Caesar. Yet we do not know these men except through others' testimony. In the order of human relations, I do not know the love of another except through his own avowal. The problem is to determine whether I can place my trust in his word. Now, there are cases where I have, not only the right, but even the duty, to trust in this word, and where it would be absurd not to do so. Inability to trust others is one of the maladies of intelligence in our day.

It is therefore legitimate under certain conditions to credit testimony as true. Are these conditions verified in the case of the testimony given by Christ? Here we are at the heart of the problem which we must undertake to solve. There is one preliminary question. It is really not worth delaying with; still, reference must be made to it, for even in this day and age we still meet people who ask it. It is the question of the historicity of Christ. It puts us in the area of historical sciences in the most commonplace sense of the word: Have we the right to consider the Gospels, St. Paul's Epistles, and the Acts of the Apostles as documents of a historicity sufficient to warrant our reliance on them for our assertion that a Jesus of Nazareth actually existed, and lived in Galilee? There is no doubt about it in the mind of any scholar of standing. And discoveries during recent years (I am thinking especially of the Qumran finds, with which I am personally occupied[4]) in fact confirm the validity of the data presented to us in the Gospels.

But this brings us, as a second step, beyond the Apostles' assertions about Christ, to what constitutes the very foundation

---

[4] Cf. Jean Daniélou, S.J., *The Dead Sea Scrolls and Primitive Christianity* (Baltimore, Helicon Press), 1958.

of our faith—Christ's own assertions about himself. Here the problem is to determine whether Christ is so reliable a witness that, when he tells us that he is God come among men (an assertion, we repeat, in itself incredible) we have a right to believe him—not only a right, but a duty. We have to be able, I mean, to say to our associates: "If you examine the problem objectively, you will be led to submit to the truth of what I am telling you; this is not a subjective opinion, but a reality which, I can honestly assure you, anyone in good faith will be brought to agree with."

What are the data in question? There is one thing that by and large the whole Gospel testifies to; that is that Christ presented himself not simply as a man, but as coming from God, and as being of the same order as God. That he did so is a primary fact, scientifically established. We are not here taking his discourses as evidence, for if it were a question of these alone, they could always be called into question, and parts pointed to as interpolations; no, we are taking the whole of Christ's behavior, during his entire life. What we are saying is that the life of Christ is inexplicable if he was not claiming for himself divine nature and divine authority. What I mean by that is that the public life of Christ was one long, constant conflict with the Jews. Now, the sole motive of the Jews' hostility towards Christ was the accusation of blasphemy brought against him. This accusation is the great witness to the divinity of Christ, because it was rendered by his adversaries, the testimony given by an adversary always being less suspect of complicity.

This accusation of blasphemy, which the Jews never stopped bringing against Christ, reveals in effect that one thing is certain, namely, that Christ never stopped claiming for himself an authority equal to God's. Two or three examples of this claim will suffice here. In the Sermon on the Mount Christ said: "You have heard that it was said, An eye for an eye and a tooth for a tooth. But I tell you that you should not offer resistance to injury." Have heard that it was said by whom? By Yahweh, who had given the Decalogue on Sinai. Christ, therefore, was claiming for himself an authority equal to Yahweh's. Some years ago a rabbi said something to me which I have often quoted since: "You see, there is just one thing that we Jews have against Christ, and that is that he altered the Law. For the Law was given by God. And only God can alter what he has set forth." My response was: "You could say nothing that would please me more. I shall borrow your whole argument. The Law was set forth by God; only God can alter what was set forth by God. Therefore, if Jesus believed he had a right to alter the Law, it must be that Jesus considered himself to be God." The rabbi was giving me one of the most striking demonstrations of the divinity of Christ, or at least was giving me iron-clad proof that there is one thing absolutely certain, and that is that Christ represented himself to be God.

Well, then, there are three solutions possible. One, he was a visionary, a mystic of some sort lost in the clouds and fancying himself God among men. Two, he was a liar; this thesis was sustained once, in the eighteenth century. Or, three, he was telling the truth, and, extraordinary though it seem, had the right to call himself the Son of God. Just three attitudes may be taken towards Christ as presented in the Gospels: putting him down as a madman, or else as a liar, or acknowledging, with all the improbability of the claim, that he was right. The tragedy of the Jewish people was that they had no other possible choice than to believe in him or to condemn him to death. For if Christ had not the grounds for calling himself the Son of God, he was a monster of pride. And from the Jewish point of view he committed the worst of transgressions, a sacrilege which, no less for us today, is the greatest of all sacrileges, a man's ambition to make himself God. The greatness of Judaism, like the greatness of Islam, lies in its denouncing idolatry, in its insisting that "God alone is God," in its denouncing man's every pretention to make himself God. The only problem is to determine whether there is not *one* case, a unique case, when a person who was a man had the right to say that he was God.

Now, is it possible to say that Christ was a madman, or a liar? There is one thing on which all men are in agreement, whether Christians, Jews, Moslems, Hindus, or even atheists, and that is that Jesus represents, at the very least, one of the very highest peaks of human nature. There are few men who do not love Christ. Gandhi considered him the greatest figure in human history. Mohammed, in the Koran, assigned him an elevated place, and saw in him the greatest of the prophets. The Jewish writer Edmond Fleg has given us an admirable work representing Jesus as seen by the wandering Jew. And numerous are the Jews today—witness Robert Aron's recent book—who consider Christ one of the most marvelous men whom the race of Israel has produced. A socialist like Barbusse wrote a book presenting Christ as one of the most admirable figures in the brotherhood of mankind. Thus, all men without exception are united in saying that Christ represents one of the peaks, and doubtless the highest peak, of human history. Is it possible to say at the same time that this man was a liar or a madman?

Since it is absolutely certain that on the human level Christ represented himself as being God, and since it is absolutely certain that on the human level he was one of the most admirable figures in human history, then this problem confronts every man: That Christ was God is perhaps improbable; yet it would be a serious matter to reject Christ's testimony. If I refuse to accept his testimony, then no human witness is worthy of belief. For if I have no right to believe Christ, whom have I grounds for believing? And I therefore do have the right, in all conscience, with clear mind and with full intellectual rigor, to say: "What Christ said is in fact improbable; and yet I must consider that he seems to me a witness of such genuineness that I have the right, on grounds of faith in his testimony, to believe the improbable."

I must add that up to this point I have restricted myself to a field accessible not only to a Christian, but also to a Jew, a Moslem, or any man. In what I have said until now, I have included nothing which calls faith into play, nothing that cannot be accepted by any just man. Thereafter comes the final and decisive step, whereby I shall see in Christ not only human testimony such as appears to me a guarantee of credibility, but the very word of God made man. The adherence of my intelligence in its supreme expression will rest upon God's very word as upon an absolutely unshakable rock. At that moment I shall make my act of faith, commit my intelligence absolutely on the testimony of Jesus Christ, and have found an unshakable position from which I can confront all difficulties, all objections, and all doubts.

I shall add, finally, that Christ has given as a mission to his Church the transmitting of this testimony from generation to generation. The Church is nothing other than a group of men officially delegated by the Trinity with the duty of announcing perpetually, to all men, without exception, the coming judgment and the salvation given by Christ to enable them to do penance. The Church in particular speaks to Khrushchev, to Mao Tse-tung, to Nehru, to Nasser, to the chiefs of state of all the world. The Church has the duty, perpetually, to tell all men what concerns every man without exception. And this testimony, when we have studied it throughout the two thousand years during which we have seen it developed, when we have seen its permanence throughout all the vicissitudes of the individuals who have borne it, when we have seen its fecundity in the souls of the saints, will then appear, itself, something so solid that we cannot fail to acknowledge in it the work of God nor to feel that we have an absolute right to place trust in it.

We are not here preaching our own ideas. We are simply saying to those around us: "I give you my assurance that here is something real, something to which you ought to be attentive, something which is truly essential in a man's life. And this I tell you because I love you and because I sincerely desire to see you share the discovery which has been mine." In such a case, the witness we bear has nothing about it of any sort of propaganda, or of any sort of intrusion into the lives of others; it is simply the desire to share the evidence of what we live by, the ultimate certitude which we possess ourselves.

I shall conclude by answering a final objection. I recall a meeting where once upon a time an eminent professor of the Sorbonne told us: "What puts me off about the faith is a certain comfortableness, something a thought middle class, something a shade like having arrived as regards one's thinking." Is it absolutely sure that what kept that man from being a Christian was the fear of comfort? Is it an absolutely sure thing that it is more comfortable to be Christian than to be not Christian? As for me, I am not persuaded of that at all. What I am convinced of, in contrast, is that the condition of a Christian, to the extent that being a Christian means agreeing to be at the disposition of someone else, is something extraordinarily uncomfortable! And you know it very well. When it comes right down to it, what puts you off is that once you set the wheels rolling you don't know how far you're liable to go. No, this, we know very well, is what keeps those without faith from having faith. And it is also what keeps those who do have faith from having more faith. We know, as Rivière put it so well, that "love involves staggering complications." We are always taking something upon ourselves when we introduce somebody else into our life, even from the human point of view. We know that no longer shall we be altogether our own man. Therein lies the adventuresomeness of human love as well as the self-sacrifice involved in it. When it comes down to it, if a man wishes to be undisturbed, he just has to give up the notion of marrying. Well, then! To allow Christ to enter our life is a terrible, terrible, terrible risk. What will it lead to? And faith—is precisely that.

So, no one will ever bring me to believe that faith is some kind of comfort. To take Christ seriously means allowing the irruption into one's life of Absolute Love, and allowing one's self to be led on to heaven knows what point. And this very risk is at the same time a deliverance, for, when all is said and done, we know very well that we ultimately desire just one thing—absolute love—and in the final tally, if it despoils us of ourselves, it leads us to what is better than ourselves. This means—and this is what seems to me essential—that faith is not a way of landing on one's feet at the end of intellectual adventures, a sort of quiet one rewards one's self with after intellectual turmoil. Faith is not an end. It is a beginning. It introduces our intelligence into the most marvelous of adventures, into what is its real destiny, namely, one day to contemplate the Trinity. It is a magnificent act in which, sensing the limits of our own understanding, we allow the uncreated Word of God to seize our intelligence and elevate it above itself to enable it to breast its highest hills.

Nor will this adventure ever have an end. The Church is magnificently optimistic enough to hold that the faith will seize us to wrest us from our individual slaveries and catch us up in an adventure which will fill our eternity and will consist in the ever more astonished discovery of the living God. How this is supposed to have some kind of taint of middle-class life or of comfortableness I just can't say.

CHAPTER VII

The
Mystery
of Life
and Death

CHRISTIAN REVELATION is not one explanation among others which man has given himself of the riddle of his existence. Nor is it, as some people have imagined, the projection of our aspirations into a fantastic heaven which only reflects back to us our own image in larger size. No, it reveals us to ourselves and thus discloses to us what we did not know that we are. It introduces us into a new dimension of existence. This is outstandingly true of our resurrection. This is not some conception of survival in which man's aspiration for immortality finds expression. It consists neither of what we call life nor of what we call death. But it reveals to us what real death is and what real life is. For Pascal was right when he said: "Take away Christ, and we know neither what death is, nor what life is, nor what God is, nor what we ourselves are."

The resurrection reveals to us first what death is. In ordinary language, death is the separation of soul and body. It is the end of this present life. In remote times men thought that it led one into a kind of diminished life. And terror at the prospect of death was terror at the thought of the mysterious world lying beyond the grave. Thus we find Antigone saying farewell to the light. Men of our time are more inclined to see death as an annihilation. More materialistic than their ancestors, they can imagine nothing more for them in a situation where the senses have no longer anything to seize upon. In either case, for both of these, the real life is the present one, and the only wish is to prolong it as many years as possible.

Now, the resurrection reveals to us that we are mistaken. The opposition between life and death is not the opposition between the present life and life after what we call death. All—all—of this pertains to one same realm of reality, which is death. For death is not the separation of soul and body. It is the separation of man from God. It defines a certain state of man which is what St. Paul called "the flesh," which is synonymous with death. The flesh does not mean the body; it is man whole and entire, soul and body, in the state of destitution. And this destitution is the condition of man left to himself, deprived of the energies of God. That state is the death of the soul, bereft of the powers of grace. And it is the death of the body, which is mortality itself.

So the present life is already a death, inasmuch as it is a life pledged to death, as Heidegger so clearly saw. And what we call death is nothing but the continuation of this dead life, only in a state of more advanced decomposition. Between the two, there is no real difference in level. For this reason, all human hopes which are centered only on the prolonging of this life leave us imprisoned in death. As for the hope that science may one day succeed in prolonging life indefinitely, this will mean only prolonging a life which is a death. The Fathers of the Church grasped this very well; they saw in death an invention of God's love to keep death from being immortal. And Simone de Beauvoir rediscovered the same intuition, showing us, in *Tous les hommes sont mortels*, the ennui that would be bred of the ceaseless repetition of biological existence as experienced by a man capable of evading death.

As for hope of survival beyond the grave, if this survival is nothing but the endless prolongation of a dead life, it is the very definition of hell. This very conception of the life here-after was what rendered the ancients' horror of death so tragic. For in their view—saner than our contemporaries'—the life beyond was indeed a life indefinitely continued, but a pale replica, among the asphodels of Hades or the shadows of Sheol, of what life on earth had been. Whence the melancholy which Father Festugière shows us haunting the whole of the ancient world, and its frenzied pleasures, which were but the other face of its despair.

Thus our destitution is greater than we thought. Death keeps a prison underground, and already in this life its door clangs upon us. Nor can any human force, nor might, nor wit wrench its brazen bars nor spring that iron door that keeps us enjailed. Mankind is in a state of captivity deeper than any economic or social slavery. This tragic reality is one that the false optimisms of our day refuse to see. Their lying hopes are the shabbiest of the ruses that turn us aside from the way of salvation. How much more sincere in this matter are the pessimists who acknowledge that man is betrothed to death and that by this very fact life is absurd. They are right in recognizing that there is no human way out of the tragedy of mortals. They are wrong in thinking that there is no way out at all.

For if the resurrection reveals to us what death is, it also reveals to us what life is. Just as death is not the life beyond death, so life is not the life this side of death. The latter, this present life, is a dead life. Nor is life the powerful current of biological life running through the animal species and the human species. The life which dissolves man in the life-flow of the species is more a tomb than a mother, as Vigny said so well. Its course is laden with corpses and bears only on its foremost waves a thin fringe of the living. Optimism over biological life strikes us as gigantic mummery, as woefully mistaken idealization of the cruel realism of biological existence.

But the true life is quite different. The true life is that of man whole and entire when he is lifted out of the corruptibility of biological existence and transformed by the divine energies which communicate incorruptibility to him. This life is the one which St. Paul calls "spirit" in opposition to "flesh." Man is spirit in his soul when this is lifted out of the emptiness of merely natural thoughts and feelings and invested with those divine habits which are called faith, hope, and charity. Man is spirit in his body when the might of the Spirit, seizing his frail flesh, lifts it out of its destitution and mysteriously enriches it with incorruptibility.

This life is the one for which man was destined in the beginning. For the Bible teaches us that God, after forming man from the slime of the earth, led him into Paradise. Now this means that, from the beginning, man has been called to partake of incorruptible life. Paradise is the place divine, instinct with the life-giving energies of the Spirit, to be restored to us in the Church. In Paradise grows the Tree of Life, which supplies the body with immortality. In God's design there exists no human race except the one called to supernatural life. For this reason, without this supernatural life man is not fully man. There is no humanism but Christian humanism. Man without God is maimed in the essential part of himself; he is the wretched residue left in the sea marshes when the tide retires, he is an empty cartridge case, a cracked and windless bellows.

The life which is indeed life is our vocation. And here is

where the resurrection reveals to us our grandeur after having disclosed to us our wretchedness. Not for death were we destined. And yet this life is not something we can come by all by ourselves. By nature we are children of wrath. The situation of mankind left to itself is a desperate one, with no way out. It is bereft of life. It is shut up in death's jail. There is in it, but beyond it—beyond it, yet short of God, in a world misshapen, but definite for all that, where we but creep ahead— a venemous root, a poisoned spring, a mystery of evil, the might of Satan, the prince of death.

To deliver mankind, no moral preachment, then, nor any economic transformation is enough. Evil is something that cannot be righted by human means. It is not a problem, it is a mystery. A problem is something we can solve, something that can be straightened out. Now, the flaw of your modern systems, of marxism or of secularism, is the belief that the mystery of man can be cleared up by rules or by revolutions. And of these two, I must say the marxists seem to me the least pharisaical. Yet theirs is not the lesser legerdemain. And they are also incurably superficial. Man does not need good advice; he needs salvation.

That was why, in the fulness of time, the eternal Word of God, who is substantial life and who has life in himself, came down into the world and into the domain of the Prince of this world. He descended into the deepest reaches of desolation, down into a point which is beyond man's range. He was a prisoner of death. And there was a moment when death thought, "Now have I won utter victory, for in the grip of my power I hold my supreme adversary." That was the bitter hour of Good Friday. But descending into the womb of death, the Word of Life destroyed the power of death, blasting evil in its mysterious root. And the sun of Easter found him stalking from hell, having burst the bars of bronze and forced the iron gates, freeing forever from death all believers in the resurrection.

Men can of course free man from certain varieties of slavery by their inventions and by their legislative programs. But the essential slavery—that of death—they cannot touch. Only Christ can do battle with the Prince of Darkness. The mystery of Easter is the mystery of this struggle. Life and death faced each other in a mighty duel. There took place, beyond man's reach, the destruction of what is beyond man's reach and to which man is captive; at the same stroke there took place the communication to man of what is beyond man and which saves man. For man's life lies in seeing God. That is why the resurrection—which is this victory and this gift—is the essential event in the history of man. Only the Lamb who was slain can break the seven seals of the book wherein lay hid the secret of our fate.

For Christ wrested the victory from death for the whole of humankind. In him came life eternal to touch the outstretched corpse to restore its life. And from then on there has been in our race a life-giving force, a divine sinewing which from the risen body of Christ tends to propagate itself in the fulness of the whole, like a yeast raising a dough, like a flame setting afire the whole bush. "I am come to set fire to the earth, and what will I but that it be kindled?" This fire of the Holy Spirit has caught at one point of human nature and he wishes it to spread to the whole, so that all will be aflame with the conflagration of love. The age of the Church is the time of this cosmic conflagration, despite all the obstacles that its enemies by their persecutions (and its friends, alas, by their tepidity) place before it.

This fire first reaches souls. It is souls first of all that the risen life of Christ engrosses in order to give life to them. The resurrection is at work in the midst of us, bearing its wonderful fruits. It seeks to lay hold on each one of us to transform him into Christ. We must put on Jesus Christ, make his dispositions ours, let the Gospel reach every sinew of our soul. The risen life is life according to the Gospel, the principle of which is the Holy Spirit. "For the love of God has been poured forth in our heart by the Holy Spirit, who was given us." The resurrection is not simply an event in the past. It constitutes our present: "If you are risen with Christ, seek the things that are on high."

But if this life seems to be still all within, this does not mean that it concerns only what is within. It must renew the whole. "Behold, I make all things new." It must have its echo, as well, the length and breadth of the cosmos. Nothing will escape its reach. Christ is living, soul and body. He will give life to our bodies, after having given life to our souls. The Word, having created all things, wishes to save all things, as well. But this cosmic resonance is still an object of hope. "Your life is hidden away with Christ, in God. When Christ, your life, appears, then you will appear also in glory." But this victory of Christ over death, as over sin, is not only a future event. In him it is already accomplished. Death is already vanquished. We await only the full realization of what is already realized in substance. The resurrection already casts its light over the whole of our existence. We are already caught up in the impetus of the resurrection, already transformed by it in baptism, already moving towards the resurrection through holiness of life, and looking forward to the consummation of the resurrection in our own bodies.

And we draw the waters of this risen life in a permanent

fashion from its living source, Christ glorified, present perpetually among us in the Eucharistic assembly. Through the
Eucharist, the glorified body of Christ, united to his soul and
to his divinity, comes in contact with our bodies and with our
souls so as to communicate this divinity to them. Addressing
the Christians of Antioch, St. John Chrysostom said that we
come back from the Eucharistic table "like lions breathing fire."
If only we had a deeper realization of the prodigious message
that is ours to bring to the world, if our lives were only better
conformed to this message, if only they testified by their
dazzling faith, by their incorruptible purity, by their devouring
love to the divine force which animates them, then surely the
walls which keep the fire of the Spirit from enkindling the
world would tumble down.

Perhaps we understand now why the resurrection is the very
core of our existence, the core of all existence. It is the sole
answer to the sole problem. This is not a question of some
fanciful speculation about the hereafter, but of our whole life,
the life of present time as well as life eternal. With justice
St. Paul argued, "If Christ be not risen, vain is our faith." It
is to this real meaning, the only real meaning, of life that we
must testify among the men of our time, through our words and
through our lives. Christ is risen, and we are alive with him.

CHAPTER VIII

Truth
and
Unity

DIVISION AMONG Christians is a tragedy. And of this tragedy we are acquainted with the essential plot. Christ desired unity for his Church. Division is a victory won within the City of God by the world. Division has its source in sin, the sin of those in the Church and the sin of those separated from the Church. It has as its result the enfeebling of the Church in its missionary work and in the testimony that it bears. For all these reasons, Church unity constitutes a real problem.

Yet, on the other hand, ecumenicism provides open range for confusions and equivocations. We find together under that brand questions which are of quite different orders: the question of collaboration of all Christians on the social or humanitarian level, the question of legitimate differences of temperament which have their place in Catholicity, and the question of the constitutional elements of unity which are a part of the deposit of faith bequeathed us by Christ. Now, any dialogue among Christians makes no sense save as conducted along clear lines, for union cannot come about save in truth.

I shall turn therefore at once to what seems to me the one and only question presented. It is absolutely not a question of an opposition between Protestantism and Catholicism as two different views of Christianity. This is a question real enough.

We shall return it. It is a question of differences. But those differences are perfectly compatible with unity of faith. They are even the essence of Catholicity. A Catholic will always refuse to see in Catholicism one particular conception of Christianity. Within these terms, it is not a question of conversion of Catholics to the Protestant "spirit" nor of Protestants to the Catholic "spirit." Such a question strikes me as bereft of meaning.

The one real question is the question of Jesus Christ. The whole debate hinges on determining what total obedience to Jesus Christ implies. It is in the measure that the fulness of Jesus Christ is recognized that unity is found existing in fact. The whole question then is to determine what the fulness of Jesus Christ implies, and not to determine whether the biblical mentality is preferable to the Scholastic mentality, or whether propheticism is more important than authority. People are not Protestants because they have a liberal temperament, nor Catholics because they have a taste for authority. Or anyhow, if they are so, they are so for the wrong reasons.

As soon as one places one's self at this angle of vision, the first thing that appears is the impossibility of speaking of a dialogue between Catholics and Protestants. For on the question of the fulness of Jesus Christ, the opposition among various Protestant groups is far greater than between these groups and Catholics. The whole spectrum of positions, then, has to be set out. That in fact is what the Oslo Lutheran professor, Einar Molland, does in his book *Christendom*, a panorama of the variety of answers given by the various Christian bodies to the question of the content of faith in Jesus Christ. He starts with Orthodoxy, which seems to him to represent the extreme tendency most opposed to Protestantism. Then he comes to Catholicism. After that, he enumerates the various positions of

Anglicanism, Lutheranism, and Churches in the Calvinist line. Last he presents the Baptist Church, the Methodist Church, and the most extreme forms of doctrinal liberalism.

It is likewise from this point of view that we can see how the World Council of Churches must lack all representative authority in the doctrinal realm. The Council's usefulness is very great in that it can co-ordinate the practical activity of the various non-Catholic bodies, and in that it does provide a meeting point for doctrinal discussions. But it is clear that it embraces Christians whose positions are radically opposed on the essential questions of faith, like whether the Church is institutional or purely confessional, or what the value of the sacraments is. But on the doctrinal level each one of the bodies which compose it is left free to dispute with the others or with the Church of Rome.

And I shall come back to what I have been saying. The only possible method is to pick one particular point and put it to the question so as to determine whether it is a part of the fulness of Jesus Christ. Then dialogue will make sense, for it will consist, not of opposing system to system, but of examining fairly what each participant considers himself bound before God to acknowledge as being part of Jesus Christ's message. The opposition is not basically one of theologies. The point is not to determine whether we prefer St. Thomas to Barth. The dialogue of theologies is part and parcel of Catholicity. There are Catholics of a Barthian temperament and Protestants of a Thomistic temperament. If that were the only question, the division would not exist. But the question is of an absolute— Jesus Christ. Nor is it a question of defending our own ideas. It is a question of the sacred trust committed by Christ to the Church which is his Spouse. The only question is to determine what makes up this deposit.

If we look at things in this way, it is clear at once that from this angle the oppositions do not have the massive character that they are sometimes given. There are in fact few dogmas which Catholics consider as making up the deposit of faith and which are not at the same time accepted by some or other representatives of the Protestant bodies. This, then, means that no dogma represents, in itself, an insurmountable obstacle, whether it be the authority of Tradition, the sacrament of holy orders, the sacrament of penance, the primacy of the bishop of Rome, or the Assumption of the Virgin Mary, for all these have been recognized as making up a part of the fulness of faith by some or other Protestant bodies.

In contrast, when Catholics, Protestants, or Orthodox believers, instead of centering the question solely on Jesus Christ, define their positions in terms of their opposition to one another, then true perspectives are dimmed out. Such is the case, to cite one typical example, with the recent article in *Réforme*, where Olivier Clément tried to construct an Orthodoxy in opposition to Catholicism and to Protestantism. This was an undertaking at second hand, foreign, as well, to the genuine Orthodox tradition, and constituting the very model of the anti-ecumenical attitude. Among the serious oppositions that go back to the fourth century, and which led to the Orthodox schism, if there is one thing clear to the eyes of history it is that dogmatic questions were quite secondary. The great Doctors of the Eastern Church are common Doctors of the universal Church.

Granted all this, it remains none the less true that the various Protestant bodies have in common the fact that they do define themselves by a common opposition to the Church of Rome. This makes us stop to think about what occasions this opposition. Now, it seems that it arises from different sources.

Historically, first of all, it is clear that at the moment when Luther appeared the Church presented a certain number of abuses which were going to have to be reformed. Of course, the principle of reform is in itself perfectly legitimate. The Church has perpetually need of reform. Just as the prophets of the Old Testament, to denounce the abuses introduced among the people of God, cited the Covenant, so there is room in the Church for a propheticism which appeals constantly to the Gospel against the infiltrations of the spirit of the world.

But, to do the Church any good, reform must possess two characteristics. On the one hand, as Father Congar has so well shown, it must bear on what is perpetually reformable, but leave intact what is irreformable. The tragedy of the Reformation is that in undertaking to suppress abuses it damaged the very substance of the faith and of the life of the Church. And on the other hand it must be carried on within the Church. Luther, of course, could legitimately agonize over the fact that his appeal for a return to the Gospel was misunderstood by the Roman curia. Francis of Assisi and Catherine of Siena agonized for the reform of the Church—but within the Church.

Here we touch the essential point. Christianity rests on two poles, the Gospel and the Church. The Church must perpetually be referred to the Gospel, but the Gospel must be perpetually lived in the Church. Fidelity to the Gospel can never be infidelity to the Church. The true, the only legitimate reform is that which has its source in love of the Church, which causes the agony of not seeing the Church so perfect as Christ would wish it, but which at no moment can be separated from the Church. For this, the unique Church, remains ever the Spouse of Christ Jesus, whatever be the sins of the men who make it up. We do have the duty of humbling ourselves; we have never the right to humble the Church.

The question of abuses bears principally on the historical

context of the Reformation. And it shows us that the sources of separation have nothing respectable about them, for they consist of sin, the sin of the men of the Church, and the sin of those who separated themselves from the Church. But a second source of opposition to Catholicism on the part of Protestant bodies lies rather in the contemporary situation. Because of the separation, Catholics and Protestants developed along different lines and tended progressively to accentuate the traits that distinguished them from each other. Protestants accentuated liberty and individualism; Catholics, authority and centralization; Protestants developed the study of the Sacred Scriptures, while Catholics placed the emphasis on the infallible magisterium of the Church. But examples are countless.

Here we find ourselves in the presence of what is doubtless today, concretely, the most obvious form of the opposition. One can speak today of a Protestant mentality and of a Catholic mentality—things that did not exist in the sixteenth century. This is noticeable in the manner of approaching questions. The Protestant appears as if always watchful against whatever might seem to take away something from the unique causality of Jesus Christ, whether it be a question of the intercession of the saints, the sacrificial nature of the Eucharist, the infallibility of the Church, or the value of merit. The Catholic, in contrast, will emphasize the reality of the gift made by Jesus Christ to the Church, to the souls of the holy, and will accentuate the fecundity of grace as giving rise to the life of the new man.

Now, on these points there are three things to be said. First, it is in this area that rapprochements seem today to be most freighted with hope. We are often reminded (so that I need not insist on the point) how receptive Catholics are today to the biblical movement, as well as, on the other hand, of modern Protestantism's rediscovery of the Church and of the sacraments. Point two, this brings us into an area where there is a question less of contradiction than of complementariness. Unity dare not be uniformity. But it must be still recognized that Protestantism and Catholicism, quite apart from properly dogmatic questions, have become opposed mentalities. As mentalities, they must acknowledge each other as complementary.

I shall further explain my thought: A Catholic cannot conceive of unity without the acceptance of what seems to him essential to the substance of the faith. There is no unity save in truth possessed in common. But in my opinion there can be no question of making Protestants accept a whole number of sociological, cultural aspects, which are historical trappings. On that level unity means reciprocal acceptance and reciprocal enrichment. And there is where the real problems arise. This does not mean that they are the easiest to resolve. For it is on this level that instinctive oppositions, hereditary repugnances, are to be found. But all of this cannot justify the rupture of the Body of Jesus Christ.

The final trait that the various Protestant bodies have in common is their refusal to acknowledge the authority of the bishop of Rome. As a matter of fact, this poses two different questions—that of the dogmatic principle involved, and that of the historical trappings of the authority at Rome. The second touches on questions we have just hinted at. The organization and the methods of the Roman Congregations, the relationship between the authority of bishops and that of the Pope—these are questions susceptible of discussion, and precisely on them the forthcoming Council may be called upon to express itself. Quite a number of venerable institutions of Christian—or medieval—origin have developed in tune with historical conditions. All the traditions (with a small letter) do not make up part of Tradition (with a capital).

A dogmatic principle, however, does exist. For a Catholic, this principle is connected with what we were speaking of on the first page of this chapter, namely, the deposit of Revelation. It is clear that this assertion is a scandal, a stumbling block, as indeed is the whole of faith. The reason why Protestants refuse to acknowledge the primacy of Peter—to the extent they see in it pretension on the part of human authority to arrogate to itself divine infallibility—is absolutely valid. It arises from the fundamental vocation of Christianity, which is the denunciation of all idolatry. It was in the name of this very principle that the Jews condemned Christ, by a legitimate sentence, inasmuch as they saw in him a man who claimed for himself, in blasphemous fashion, an authority equal to God's. The unhappy part was that, in this unique case, Jesus had the right to claim this authority for himself, because he is God. The problem is to determine whether the Church has not the right to claim this authority for itself, because it was given it efficaciously and unalienably by God, in such a way that it holds nothing from itself, but acknowledges the gift of God that was given it.

Thus finally the question centers on the history of salvation. Did sacred history continue after Jesus Christ? Is the age of the Church sacred history by the same title as the time of the Old Testament and the time of Jesus Christ? That is, ultimately, are we in a world where there exist operations properly speaking divine? The Catholic assertion is uniquely that, just as the Church really communicates the life of Christ through the sacraments, is the instrument, that is, which God uses to communicate a really divine life, just so the Church communicates divine truth through its magisterium—truth, that is, which is handled by God himself and of which the Church is only the servant. Believing in infallibility is rendering thanks to the living God who works in our midst an operation literally divine.

Now we see the double aspect of the question of unity. There is the dogmatic aspect. Unity is the acknowledgment of the fulness of Jesus Christ. It can be based only on a common credo which contains the totality of what constitutes this fulness. The Church of Rome can here only profess its faith in the fact that certain dogmas are part of this fulness. There is, on the other hand, the human aspect. There are human obstacles opposed to unity—imperialisms and particularisms. The immense task of getting rid of these obstacles is open to us. Here it will be the part of the wisdom of the forthcoming Council to show that the problem of the reform of the Church is anterior to the problem of the unity of the Churches, for it has as its object to determine what is secondary and reformable in the Church. A way has opened up; we know not where it will lead. We know only that we must set our foot on it, our only map fidelity to the truth, and our only compass nostalgia for unity. If all Christians pray and seek, God will bring about what could never be brought about by man.

CHAPTER IX

Christianity
and
Technological
Civilization

IT MAY be said that our age reveals two facts essentially characteristic of it. On the one hand, it is *the age of technology.* For ethnologists, the tool, along with rite, defines man, and it is noteworthy that it is these two traits that allow him to be recognized. But it is certain that technology assumes today, in contemporary civilization, a very special extension. One may say that it brands this civilization, at once by its application in more and more extended areas, by the accelerating pace of its development, and by its extension to all the human masses: wide sections of mankind who had remained strangers to it are no more so today, and we have yet to see what the missionary consequences of this extension are to be.

The other fact which characterizes the contemporary world is *atheistic humanism.* This is a specifically modern phenomenon, perfectly foreign to ancient civilizations, and up to now perfectly foreign as well to peoples who were at some remove from Western influence. But today the phenomenon is universal; and tomorrow the mission problem in Africa and the Far East, as it is today in the West, will be that of a world separated from God, and not simply a problem of the old religions. Indeed the question arises whether a missionary destined to go to China should study Confucius, or Karl Marx. It is obvious that even today the works of Marx would be the more important for getting to know the mentality he would be bound to face.

Is there some connection between these two facts? That is the problem. Is it technological civilization which engenders atheistic humanism? That was the thesis of Karl Marx; and it is well to recognize that in many regards it presents certain probabilities. There is sufficient chronological coincidence of the two facts that it may be wondered whether there is not something in technological civilization that constitutes an obstacle to the religious attitude. It is plain that man in our technological civilization does meet a certain number of difficulties to the religious attitude. Let me make this clear: I mean man in our technological civilization and not the scientist. The problem is that of the technological civilization which totally impregnates our contemporary mentality and not that of scientific research as such.

Must we, as a certain number of men do, conclude that technological civilization is something accursed, that as such it constitutes a deviation which will turn man aside from his supernatural vocation? Or may we, on the contrary, think that through the crisis which its development presents today it may tomorrow become a girder for a new expansion of Christianity; and under what conditions? Here is a question already serious on the theoretical level, but on the practical level actually acute, since it affects the presentation of Christ's message in a machine-age world.

What, first of all, are *the obstacles which technological civilization puts in the way of the religious attitude*, of adoration? Why may a machine-age world be in conflict with the religious attitude? For many minds today it is impossible to understand how one may be a man of the twentieth century, of the atomic age, and still a religious man. Religion seems a survival of a universe quite out of fashion. Why this outlook?

One of the traits whereby a machine civilization threatens to turn man away from adoration is that *it causes man to live in a universe made up of his own works*. Machine-age man lives surrounded by machines, tools, instruments by which he transforms his life, landscapes even which are the skylines of the great modern cities with their immense factories. Thus he finds himself surrounded by things which reflect his own image back to him from every direction. Father Dubarle remarked some time ago that one of the traits which characterizes machine-age man is that he no longer has contact with nature in its primitive state, and is in touch constantly with natural forces as these are recomposed by human ingenuity. As a result, the world of technology returns to man his own image; and in this mirror it is himself that he contemplates and himself that he admires.

This point is essential if we are to understand the mentality of a great many young people today, all enthusiastic over the discoveries and inventions of the age they live in. One has only to reflect on the mystique which was created around the invention of the Sputnik, and all the hope—and at the same time all the anguish—raised by atomic energy. In this way, the scientist seems to many young people today the great hero of the modern world, the one who holds in his hands all the secrets of power.

Now there is something serious, for if the heavens proclaim the glory of God, machines proclaim the glory of man: Modern man, it may be said, is apt to be bewitched by a kind of incantation which is that of this whole marvelous world that he finds at his finger tips and that is increasing today on an almost fabulous scale. All this gives him, in his own eyes, a more and more considerable importance and magnitude, and relegates, for him, the reality of God's operations to the background, so that his practical interest in them is decreased in proportion as his attention is centered on the operations of man. From this point of view, then, it may be said that the world of technology seems to turn man away from God.

But this is not the only aspect. Besides greatness, the world of *technology awakens in man a sense of his power*. What in fact characterizes this world is the progressive mastery which man achieves over the forces of nature, permitting him to put them to his use. When one compares the situation of primitive man, crushed by cosmic forces, with that of man of today, one grasps the feeling he has of recovering today all that he formerly gave to God simply because he was not the master of it, and of extending his conquest (certain aspects of today's science give every hope of it) indefinitely towards ever receding limits.

"A few decades from now," Father Dubarle remarks, "man will have covered essentially the whole ground in the matter of technical power over inert matter." Thus, a few decades from now we shall be able to say that man has become truly master over inert matter, understanding this not only of the terrestrial globe, but even, progressively, of the sidereal universes. And, Father Dubarle continues, "he will have advanced what he has begun in the realm of living matter." This is another direction in which progress may go ahead very rapidly, and may lead, as we can gather from our reading, to man's becoming master of his biological fate as well, to the point where this mysterious world of life, which used to be the very thing that escaped man's grasp, will be progressively mastered, this mastery permitting, as certain materialist philosophers have commenced to say, the gradual possibility of an indefinite prolongation of life. Thus man, who formerly experienced a feeling of captivity and had recourse to a *deus ex machina* to come and save him, thinks now that he himself is capable of freeing himself from this captivity and bringing about his own salvation.

And he has the feeling that recourse to something outside his world is in fact a kind of laziness; that the need is to devote all man's energies in his struggle for his own liberation; that it is man who will be the demiurge of man and will create the happy and liberated mankind of tomorrow. This is the myth which is at the bottom of marxism, which, however, only expresses systematically what exists in a more or less latent form in a good many minds.

Finally, there is a third aspect under which we may consider the world of technological civilization as creating an obstacle to religious life: It accustoms the mind to approaches very different from those by which the religious world may be attained; it counts as important values those of efficiency rather than of truth. In the realm of scientific invention one cannot properly speak of truth; there are never anything but hypotheses, which can be superseded by other hypotheses and which are verified by their concrete effectiveness. Now, this criterion tends to become the measure of all things; and *spiritual realities are denounced as lacking in pragmatic effectiveness in respect of the concrete transformation of human life.* This is one of the objectives which we find to be most current: Christianity is of no use to us for the task that lies before us, namely, the transformation of man's material conditions.

Furthermore, the scientific approach associates criteria of certitude with possibilities of concrete experimentation—something impossible in the religious realm; and the upshot is that religious assertions are felt to have a gratuitous character, and to lack the same quality of certitude as possessed by what is susceptible to experimentation. The result is that for many scientists, even those who are Christians, religion is essentially a subjective affair, which arises from feeling and cannot be objectively and rationally based. Oh, religious sentiment will be respected—life is sad enough, we are told, and it will not do to deprive men of the consolations of religion; but it will be thought that a clear-thinking mind should be capable of dispensing with this recourse and of facing up to truth in all its unremitting coldness.

Note moreover that the scientific approach is essentially that of invention. It consists in going always ahead, in progressing; the world of science is a world of perpetual discovery. In such a climate, announcement by religion of a word which has been spoken once and for all, assertion of a truth with an absolutely permanent character—this will easily appear as contrary to the life of the mind. Now what we remark here—no less than what we have remarked above—would not be verified in the case of superior minds, of men who know the limits of science; but it is in fact on the level of the student in technological courses, of the specialized technician, that I am placing myself, for it is there that we find the mentality which in effect screens out religion, closes the blinds on adoration.

But there is another side to the story—the fact that technological civilization, precisely through its development, is touching certain limits, and that this fact is beginning to be felt by a certain number of our contemporaries. We are not referring to some breakdown in the technological world, but to its limits and to its insufficiency. We were saying a few pages back that what characterizes the technological world is that man discovers himself in it. But the long and short of it is that he discovers himself so much that he ends up with a kind of feeling of captivity. *The world of technology shuts man up inside man and man's powers.* As a result, he is beginning to experience that stifled feeling which brought Claudel's St. Thérèse to cry out, "A window, a window, a window to escape from everlasting vanity." For if the world of technology stretches and stretches and stretches man's prison out indefinitely, still it doesn't get him out of it; it extends things indefinitely in their own order, but it does not bring anybody into a different order.

This is already true *in the area of knowledge.* Let us take for example the sciences of man. It may be said that at present here is where the greatest strides are being made in the world of technology. But we may be sure that when everything about man has been explained, and all the wheels and springs exhibited, there remains "the I know not what and the almost nothing," which is to say that finally, when everything has been explained, there will be left over precisely the essential, what man is at the very core and which remains inaccessible to science; then the only possible step is to another order of means of investigation.

What is true of the realm of knowledge is true also of the *realm of existence,* which is to say that there are captivities for which technology can free man. It has considerably diminished the burden of human existence, and, in this sense, it has been a great undertaking. I am thinking of all that medicine, that surgery have done to alleviate human sufferings; for this one must express immense gratitude. But, here again, there are limits. There is also about technology something irremediably superficial, something that stays on a certain level and can never rise above that level. There is an essential wretchedness from which no science will ever free man—the wretchedness of death and of sin. Christ alone plumbed this spiritual wretchedness which he descended into hell, and there reached and destroyed the root of evil.

To illustrate this by an example, I shall cite the most characteristic, the limit problem which we all come up against, namely, that of death. Technical science envisages this problem. Its program would be incomplete if it ignored it. It may, then, undertake to prolong life and to push death further and further back. At the very best, it could do so indefinitely. But the existence it would thus prolong indefinitely would always remain none the less an existence mortal and corruptible, where man would trudge around endlessly in the cycle of biological existence. In contrast, the life which Christ brings us is a passage to another order of existence, that of incorruptible life, transformed by the energies of the Spirit and freed from biological servitude.

I turn now to *man's anguish over his own powers.* I am thinking here of the physicists when they became conscious that they had incarnated a deadly power with possibly tragic consequences. The man of technical science is afraid. He is afraid because today he has in his hands powers incomparably beyond any possessed by man in the past and which make it perfectly possible for him to be the instrument of cosmic catastrophe.

For scientific progress does not suffice to halt man's tragedy; something more is required than the invention of instruments; what is required is determining what to do with them. Thus today there has become salient the problem of the moral responsibility of the scientist. But the problem itself is not of today's birth. Leonardo da Vinci, who was an engineer, refused to publish the designs of the submarine he had invented, because he thought it essentially unfair to attack, without warning, an enemy who cannot see you! This presupposes that technical means are remandable to another order of values which can be nothing but a certain absolute of good and evil, a moral, humane order, only in terms of which can technology have any final sense.

Finally, an exclusively technological way of looking at the world itself *deprives it of its moral dimension*. For the cosmos is not simply an ensemble of forces which we can undertake to put to our uses. It is also a world which reveals to us something that is beyond itself. A universe of pure technology would be like a temple converted to secular purposes, a fane wherein something would be plainly missing. Now the sacred, the religious dimension of the world is a thing for which modern man has again commenced to have a kind of vital thirst. And, when it comes down to it, adoration is a need as irrepressibly human as technology; as pointed out earlier, rite is the sign of man no less that the tool. A man who does not adore at all is not a man.

What, then, are the avenues by which the modern world of technology presents possibilities of consecration? I shall say at once what technology seems to me to bring to religion, and that is a certain purification. To the extent that it recoups for man's account certain things that had been considered supernatural, *it frees religion and the supernatural from a whole cumbersome burden of the pseudo-supernatural and the pseudo-religious*. Primitive man identified the supernatural everywhere, but largely on account of his ignorance. Purification of genuine religion from such degradations results from man's investigation of the whole range of his powers. There is, therefore, in this sense, a wholly positive contribution from the technological world to the religious world.

In the second place, we were saying that technology gives man a sense of his own power, and that as a result man has been brought to hymn the glory of man and not the glory of God. But, after all, *does the glory of man not redound ultimately to the glory of God?* We need have no fear that man will be too great. Péguy remarked that there is no call to downgrade Sévère in order to exalt Polyeucte. Some people think man must be abased if God is to be magnified. I should say that, on the contrary, the greater man seems to us the more God will seem all the greater still; and, in this sense, we have nothing to fear over what is lodged to man's credit.

It is for this reason that we do not balk at giving a woman—the Virgin Mary—that extraordinarily high standing that some people reproach us for giving her on the grounds that by attributing too great greatness to the Blessed Virgin we seem to be taking something away from Jesus Christ. This appeals to us as utterly groundless, because what we attribute to the Virgin she has only received from Jesus Christ; and the greater the greatness Christ has granted to the Virgin Mary, the greater still does he appear to us. The greater man appears, the more we understand how surpassingly so must be he from whom man holds this greatness; and through the looking glass of modern man there is a new image of God which we are enabled to descry.

This very world that technology has developed may itself be sacralized; there is absolutely no reason why it cannot be capped with a temple in which God will have his dwelling, and the whole consecrated to him. Already through the resources of modern architecture, and through the new materials it has at its disposal, we see the development of a religious architecture which is like the expression of the modern soul and strikes us as one of the first beginnings of what may be a consecrated world of technology. Again, it may be said that the way man has been learning today about the dimensions of space and time, and learning to handle them, has given us a realization that both space and time are far more vast than we ever imagined them. I can think of nothing that gives me a mightier image of God, as he is manifested by means of the world, than those vast stellar spaces which the astronomy and physics of today allow us to glimpse; and we feel that our expanding world will furnish still finer images through which God will be expressed.

As has often happened in other periods of history, new forces have appeared, and, on first appearance, have seemed obstacles, but because they are new forces, and have the greenness and rawness of new growth. Once upon a time, a city seemed itself a thing accursed, and the Israelite nomads thought no salvation possible but in the open life of the desert. And yet we see a moment when history had a turning, when David built the holy city, Jerusalem, and brought God into it before bringing man there. *We, too, are at one of the turning points of history, at one of those moments marked by the presence of new forces which up till now have been in play outside the ambit of the Gospel, but about which there is no indication that they cannot be marked with the sign of the cross.* We must imagine how the world of technology will cease being an obstacle to adoration and become, instead, something positively conducive to adoration.

We have to rediscover the sacred, as an essential component of the human soul, in the dimensions which the cosmos has assumed today. That is why one of our main problems will be to discover a new symbolism, as it were. For we shall have to find a new way of discerning—in this brave new universe we are even now exploring—the new religious dimensions that fit it. There was a cosmology of the middle ages; there was a cosmology of the age of Galileo; we are entering today upon a third cosmology, and the instant problem is new representations, new paradigms, so that the essential data of religion will not be frozen in superseded representations; we shall have to be forever reinventing, it might be said, for the permanent message of religion, forms of expression corresponding to man's exploration of the universe.

This, in fact, is already on the way to accomplishment. The present-day religious resurgence is not taking place in the world of philosophers and literary men, who today are in great part prisoners of the decadent intellectuality which I decried earlier in this volume; religious resurgence today is to be found essentially in scientific circles; here there are appearing, these days, fine, enthusiastic young people, right in touch with what is most uplifting in the contemporary world, namely, the marvelous accomplishments of today's science; and they are experiencing the need to enrich technological expansion with a humanism that will give it meaning and direction. As we remarked early, science today is rediscovering man; it is rediscovering responsibility, it is discovering, by the means proper to it, the necessity of placing these means in the service of man; it is looking for a vision which will enable this magnificent scope of science to appear as centered upon a flowering of mankind and ultimately on some final sense of history such as will bring it to rediscover an absolute. Here mention must be made of the great importance in contemporary France of the work of Teilhard de Chardin. Teilhard's theses may be disputed; we are not looking to him for a new theology; but the fact remains that his work is among those which today trace the most promising lines of development of the rediscovery of religion springing up in the very heart of the technological universe.

It is noteworthy that the president of the Senegalese government, Leopold Senghor, in the constitution of Senegal was inspired essentially by the philosophy of Teilhard de Chardin. It may be said that these are the only ideas that the African nations today have to oppose to marxism as inspiration for the building of a civilization. What I think we are seeing there is really an outgrowing of marxism; marxism, of course, has not been left completely behind; but passed over it certainly has been. In another direction, we must be struck by the fact that at the present time the French Communists are trying to annex Teilhard, because they sense quite accurately that this is in fact the form of thought most harmful to them, since it retains all that is valid in enthusiastic approval of scientific expansion, but in a spiritualistic and religious sense which renders it still more rich instead of impoverishing it as marxism does by reducing it to a positivism philosophically out of date.

From this point of view, similarly, we are witnessing a rehabilitation of intelligence. I said on an early page here that intelligence is sick; the intelligence of the intellectuals I was speaking of in that connection is sick; theirs is an intelligence believing itself incapable of any use, incapable of attaining truth. But now scientific thought, for its part, believes in the intelligence and is at the same time experiencing today the limits of scientific understanding; along the very pattern of Aristotle of old, it is through physics that we are on the verge of rediscovering metaphysics. It is, then, in the course of the development of scientific thought that we are on the brink of once more emerging into a philosophy which merits the name, one, that is, which is not a cultivation of subjectivity, not an exercise of intelligence with no objective outside itself, but a search for the truth in the fulness of its expression. And it is also there that we shall perhaps rediscover happiness.

In the broader view of our civilization, one of the features of the revival of religion is the religious feeling that is stirring today at the core of human concerns; we had been making religion too much something isolated; I have a horror of the conception of religion as a private affair. Totalitarian states understand this quite well; they always make sure right away, as a first step, to restrict the domain of religion to the mere conducting of religious services, and to separate from it all the domains of intellectual life, of social life, of political life; now this move in effect ultimately destroys religion by uprooting it from the soil of human affairs. But today it is the opposite that is happening; religion is stirring again at the very base of human activities; it is springing up again in scientific thought, inasmuch as the latter, in the course of its inventory of the cosmos, is feeling the need to go beyond itself; it is springing up again within the state, inasmuch as adoration, or the presence of God, appears today to be as substantially necessary to the common weal as are economic life and scientific progress.

This fact is the one that the man of today is experiencing more and more; there is a certain false secularism, a complete split of human activities off to one side, and God off to the other side, a process that manages to kill both religion and man with one stroke. In contrast, this rediscovery of the fundamental place of the religious at the very heart of human activities is one of the rediscoveries which will build the world of tomorrow. Adoration is as necessary to a state as labor is, as the national economy is; monasteries of contemplative men and women are as necessary to the state as are factories; man, human society, can no more dispense with the bread of God than with the bread of man. And I think that it is in this vital perspective that there will appear—and perhaps exactly where we should not expect it, precisely, that is, in a world which has too long been deprived of God—new wellsprings of religion.

CHAPTER X

Truth
and
Society

IT IS something very disappointing to find so often, in big national or international meetings of some kind, eminent men giving evidence of a remarkable intelligence when talking about their specialty—economics, jurisprudence, science, whatever it may be—and then being satisfied with the vaguest commonplaces as soon as they touch upon what are usually spoken of as "spiritual values." One gets the feeling that for them, if science is the realm of precision, spiritual values make up the realm of imprecision. This metaphysical asthenia, this confusion of mind when the essential is touched on, constitutes without doubt one of the main weaknesses of the Western world. Now, spiritual values are susceptible of quite as rigorous precision as scientific data.

Precision, then, must be brought to these values. Eighteenth-century thought, in its confidence in the perfectibility of human nature, made liberty the principle of political and economic life. This was developed in a twofold direction. On the one hand, on the economic level, individual liberty in production and exchange was presented as the mainspring of the growth of prosperity. On the other hand, on the political level, the popular will, as expressed through universal suffrage, was considered the source of law: This was the doctrine of *Le contrat social*. Now, under both aspects, this philosophy of liberty resulted in failures which made plain the need for some rethinking.

Under the first aspect, the danger appeared in the form of the advantage gained by one of the components of economic life at the expense of the others. It is perfectly true that a certain economic liberty is among the just demands of a free world. Without a minimum of this liberty, spiritual liberties cease to be guaranteed. But economic society involves another pole, which is the common good. If it is the state's duty to insure the free exercise of every liberty, and hence of economic liberty, it must also take care that this liberty is not exercised to the exclusive profit of a few and at the expense of the whole. In reality, pure economic liberalism is an ideology which sets up one aspect of the economy as an absolute.

These reflections invite us to go a bit deeper. What we are defending when we defend man's freedom is not a liberal ideology as against a socialist ideology; it is a challenge to all political ideologies insofar as they set up certain elements of temporal society as absolute. We think, in fact, with Raymond Aron, that these ideologies are the source of present-day humanity's worst evils. They constitute the secular religions of a world which, having ceased to look for the absolute where it is, which is to say over and beyond politico-economic society, projects it onto this society, where it does not belong. One of our essential tasks is, in the words of Jeanne Hersch, "to rinse political economy of every adulteration of the absolute."[5]

It must be clear that the first thing we must avoid is falling into the error of erecting false absolutes in our adherence to a liberal ideology. This does not mean, at all, that we are not obliged to defend economic liberty. Indeed, one of the faults

[5] Jeanne Hersch, *Idéologies et réalité,* p. 23.

we find with communist society is failure to value this liberty. But we defend it, not as a new Gospel, from which we are to expect salvation, but as just one component of economic society, with the common good as its counterpart. Then we are in the field of realities, not the field of ideologies. Nor does this mean that we reject absolute values; it means that we refuse to do what we blame communism for doing—finding them where they do not exist.

The problem posed by liberty as the foundation of law is different, but it likewise calls for some distinctions. Here again, it is plain that, more than any other, the democratic conception of the state calls for the exercise of liberty. This does not mean that that conception is incompatible with other kinds of government, wherein the executive power may be more or less strong. But that is not the question we are considering here. If the democratic ideal is in fact valid, it is often accompanied by a philosophy which tends in practice to destroy it. This political philosophy is the one which makes the popular will the very source of right, of law, and not simply the designation of its modality.

This juridical voluntarism is in fact doubtless at the bottom of the principal errors against which we must take a stand. The moment the popular will appears as the supreme and infallible arbiter, nothing is to prevent its making what is right coincide with its own will to exist. And that is in fact what happens. Nationalism under its modern form is the first expression of this error. But Brugmans has denounced this nationalism as one of the greatest obstacles to the ideal of the European community.[6] We are not speaking here of patriotism as a basic feeling, nor of the right of nationalities as a people's legitimate aspiration for independence, nor yet of the sovereignty of the

[6] L. F. Brugmans, *Les Origines de la civilisation européenne*, pp. 51–54.

state, but of the ideology which makes the national will an absolute. John Nef, in his book on war and human progress, showed how the attribution of this sovereign character to the nation sponsored the modern type of ideological wars.

It is the same principle which, taken up by marxism, makes the will of the proletariat an absolute. The popular will then becomes the instrument of the worst sorts of oppression. It issues within in totalitarianism and the strangulation of liberties, and without in ideological war. It is thus found to destroy democracy. And that is why we are led to dissociate democracy as a political reality from a philosophy of political liberty ordinarily associated with it, and to look instead for its true foundations. For my part I am not in agreement with Hans Kohn when he writes that "modern Western civilization, through its emancipatory mobilization, is becoming the greatest revolutionary force in human conditions, in fact, the permanent revolution."[7] It has perhaps been that. But then it unleashed in the world the very forces which menace it itself today. And this must place on it the duty of inquiring whether it ought not to verify its foundations.

If the national will, or the will of a class, does not create right, and cannot determine good and evil by decree, this is because there exists a higher court, to which one can appeal against it. One of the essential principles of a just society appears here: it is anti-totalitarian, which is to say that it refuses to make the state the supreme tribunal. Yet this has no sense save as one can appeal against the state to a higher seat of justice. This appeal is to the existence of an order which may be called human nature, the right of the human person, which has a permanent, universal character—the existence of a system of values which is not at the mercy of the whim of

[7] Hans Kohn, *Communauté Atlantique, Cahiers de Bruges*, 1937, p. 17.

individuals, or of communities either, but is, instead, imposed on all as an absolute.

This point is one of those on which it seems that a consensus might best be established. In the final report of the commission on religion and spiritual values of the Congress of Bruges, the first proposition is "the respect for the intrinsic worth of the human person, a value which transcends every absolute and idolatrous conception of the state."[8] The very notion of person implies an end value, and imposes an unconditional respect. But there is more to it than that. It implies a destiny which transcends political or economic society, making man something more than a cell of the social organism, and implying, in the words of John of the Cross, that "one of man's thoughts is worth more than all the universe." This does not mean that the human person does not have to submit to the legitimate requirements of society; but it implies that society, in turn, exists only to aid man to attain his end—an end that lies beyond society.

We must note that this assertion of the worth of the human person implies, if it is not to be hypocrisy, a duty towards every human being. Not only does it constitute a condemnation of every racism and every nationalism, but it implies a positive obligation to help all men to reach a truly human condition. Let me turn again to the Bruges resolutions: "Liberty is inseparable from human solidarity and from the duty to give all men access progressively to material and spiritual goods." That to which everything must be referred is the community of persons. This likewise implies world-wide application of these principles. In this sense, the problem of the undeveloped countries is an ethical problem of the first importance.

This brings us to the answer we were aiming for earlier when we asserted that liberty is the principal reference of civilization.

[8] *Ibid.*, p. 120.

We acknowledged this liberty first on the level of political and economic life. But we noted that its roots must be sought elsewhere, for if it be considered only on this level, it is in danger of destroying itself. And indeed the import of liberty which we arrive at is that of the human person precisely as transcending the political or economic community. That is spiritual liberty, of which a Berdyaiev has magnificently exalted the sovereign independence from all temporal ends, because its destiny is spiritual.

We shall note that this implies all-important consequences for the political and economic realm as such. We have often remarked that the error of contemporary ideologies has been to exaggerate the importance of political affairs by transforming them into a secular religion—whence come intolerances, tyrannies, wars. Political affairs must be put back in their place. The political is essentially the realm of the contingent, inasmuch as its object is to balance complementary elements. It is the realm of compromise (not necessarily of principles, but of measures). Jeanne Hersch has clearly shown that the political as such does not create values, but "a void where something is possible."[9] From this no man's land one may never expect a great deal of good; but it can prevent a great deal of harm.

This is why political and economic activity is essential, but inasmuch as it renders something else possible, and not because it itself is something final. One of the worst forms of deviation communism has given the modern world is the turning of all problems into political ones. Philosophical, religious, and artistic values are no longer considered save in their political implications. Thus, by a tragic subversion, it is the political line which becomes the absolute reference, and all the rest becomes relative. It is the contrary operation which we must

[9] Jeanne Hersch, *op. cit.*, p. 97.

accomplish. We must restore the primacy to the values of truth, of beauty, of spirituality, and to the whole vast domain of the private life of man, and domain of work, of love, and of religion. The very purpose of the political is to render this possible. To borrow the metaphor of a Christian writer of old, Hermas, political economy is the arbor, itself sterile, but to which clings the vine, which does bear fruit.

We may also observe that if politics is not the source of moral and spiritual values, neither is morality sufficient to make good politics. Of course, here again, it is clear that political activity must be inspired by purposes proper to man, and that in this sense it must submit to morality. But otherwise it moves in the domain of the relationship of forces which constitute the law of human societies. As Jeanne Hersch remarks, politics cannot be pure Macchiavelli, but neither can they be pure Kant. It is society's duty, in the name indeed of the spiritual values it must safeguard, to be able to defend them on the plane of political realism. There can exist a pseudo-evangelical pacifism which would mean the betrayal of spiritual values.

Thus, human history can be expressed neither in terms of a pure battle of wild beasts nor in terms of a reign of morality. It is an effort to make moral values triumph, but in a world which is also one of a combination of forces. In political economy, power is an essential element as well as law, as Ernest Lefever has ably shown. And this is bound up with the very essence of temporal society, with the contingent nature of political elements, which are never wholly permeable to morality. Economic, demographic, and political entities constitute the context within which conditions of balance must be sought out. Conscientious objectors, who represent the extreme degree of political idealism, often seek an argument in the early

Christians' refusal of military service. But Hans von Campen-hausen has shown that this did not prevent early Christians from praying for the armies which guarded the frontiers of the Empire.[10] And when the Empire became Christian, Christians found that they had to assume responsibility for the state, and from that moment on normally assumed military obligations.

This shows us again the limited character of political society, and the danger of projecting messianic aspirations on it, of expecting more from it than it can give. Precisely there lies the error of all the secular religions, be they liberal or totalitarian. By turning minds from real political tasks, they falsify political realities. One of our essential tasks is to denounce myths, whether the creation of naive optimism or instruments of clever propaganda, whether illusions or lies. For the one is as dangerous as the other. One of the features of genuine political economy is what I shall call by a name pretty well forgotten today—the spirit of *measure*, of moderation, of wisdom.

To win an ear for moderation is doubtless one of the difficulties. For it is easier to arouse enthusiasm with myths than to set realistic, hence necessarily limited, goals for political programs. Is what Admiral Redford in November of 1955 called "the free world ideology" what we have to oppose to Communist ideology? Must we enter upon psychological warfare? Is our goal what the New York *Herald Tribune* called a "Marshall Plan of ideas"? Are we here the children of light, representatives of the good, as against the children of darkness, representatives of evil?

Who does not see that to accept such a point of view would

---

[10] Hans von Campenhausen, "Der Kriegdienst der Christen," *Festschrift für Karl Jaspers*, pp. 255–264.

be to fall into the very error which we must denounce? To do so would be to make a secular religion of democracy, to give a religious character to political values, to accept the attitude which the communist world seeks to bring us around to. Ours is the opposite task of ridding the political of its pseudo-religious content. And in this we are faithful to our ideal, which is to proclaim that the true destiny of the person is realized beyond any earthly state, in what Christians call the Kingdom of God and which is, at least for all free men, the kingdom of the spirit, the society of persons. In a remarkable chapter of his book *Ethics and United States Foreign Policy* the American theologian Ernest Lefever studies this question of the war of words and of ideas.[11] He shows in how far such warfare is legitimate. And it is true that we must have confidence that we are fighting for the defense of values which merit defense. But he also emphasizes the danger of a buildup of political ideology easily turning into a propaganda which empties words of their meaning, peace and liberty becoming empty words that no longer fool anybody, and which finally ends up in justifying anything and everything.

For our part, we refuse to oppose one myth to another. We refuse to promise a paradise on earth. Though this may place us in a minority, we believe that, in the end, truth will have the last word. It is because we believe in human values, and wish to defend them, and because words do have a meaning for us that we refuse to put these values at the service of political propaganda. Yet it is plainly true, on the other hand, that political activity should serve these values. A civilization becomes enfeebled when it no longer lives the values which are its reason for being. The enemy that lies in wait for it is then within rather than without. And doubtless our quest is for

[11] Pp. 134–161.

realization of what we ought really to defend, for this constitutes for us values apart from which life is not worth living.

Thus the proclamation of the transcendence of the human person over political and economic society seems to us the essential element of civilization. But this remains negative. This order which is not the political order, to which the spiritual person belongs, which he considers the highest court of appeal, and in the name of which he claims the right to judge political institutions, can be more completely identified. It implies a derivation from an absolute among values, for, as we have already stated, human liberty is not the source of right, but is derived from a good and a true which exist outside it and to which it is referred. Concretely this order of values corresponds to the Judaeo-Christian revelation.

If we reconsider the principal themes which we have selected for treatment so far, it is in fact in the Judaeo-Christian perspective that they assume their meaning. As we said, right is not the arbitrary creation of the collective will, but corresponds to a law which is imposed on man and which he is not free to alter according to his wishes. Now, this implies for liberty the recognition of a value by which it recognizes that it can be limited without being abolished. This limit, which compels recognition as meriting absolute respect, and which does not have its source in man's will, can be only a higher will, exacting acknowledgment as worthy of absolute reverence and adoration. The moral absolute implies an element of the sacred. This the believer acknowledges in the living God. But the agnostic, the moment he recognizes this sacred character of the moral law, acknowledges this absolute, nameless though it is to him.

Similarly, respect for the human person appears as having its ultimate basis in the fact that he is called to a destiny which transcends terrestrial existence. Only thus does his transcendence of political society assume its full meaning. The community of persons is no mere abstract society, but the concrete reality of that future city with which the present world is in labor. The revelation of the infinite value of the human person has its source in, and preserves its full meaning only in the revelation, given us in the Gospel, of God's love for every man. To this point Greek thought did not arrive. That is why it is legitimate to say with the English historian Douglas Jerrold (whom I find cited in Allen Tate's volume on culture and revelation), that Christian civilization is not one civilization among others, but the only one built on the rights of the human person, rights deriving from faith in the immortality of man's soul.

CHAPTER XI

Truth
and
the
Individual

THE QUESTION of the balance a Christian ought to strike between his Christian vocation on the one hand and his duties in the world on the other has been a particularly vexing one for a good score of years now. It presents itself on more than one level, and first of all on the practical level. Christians formerly, Christians in the nineteenth century, were reproached for not grasping the importance of terrestrial values and for considering the Christian vocation too exclusively as an eternal one, with the result that they were not interested in human problems, in the development of society, and in the need for co-operating in its progress. To this disincarnate Christianity has been opposed what is styled incarnational Christianity, with the idea that what is called greater engagement is to be henceforth the rule (these words, leitmotifs of thinking on the subject, have tended to become slogans these past few years).

Still, difficulties have arisen here, too. In this engagement in terrestrial duties, would not the Christian, at the opposite extreme, run the danger of reducing his Christianity to the building up of what is no lasting city, and of turning these terrestrial values into an absolute? Would this incarnational Christianity not then become a pure humanism, delicately

141

united with Christianity? I recall a discussion I had once upon a time with Merleau-Ponty, on the subject of an article in which he had explained that Christianity was fortunately in the process of undergoing an evolution, of changing, he said, from a Christianity of transcendence to an incarnational Christianity, consisting in God's becoming more and more man; but this, in his scheme of thought, meant that it was thenceforth man who was becoming God, which is not quite exactly the Christian theology of the Incarnation. And one can see, in fact, where this evolution sometimes succeeded in leading: to the leaving aside of the divine element in Christianity, seeing in it only its human element, and making Christianity into a certain form of humanism.

Are we forced to choose between transcendence and incarnation? Between God and man? Or must we speak, as some people do, of a divided loyalty, wherein our life is torn between God, tugging at the one side, and man, tugging at the other? Between the attraction of contemplation, which solicits us to leave aside all human things so as to be free for the things of God, and, in the opposite direction, a social duty demanding our exclusive attention to terrestrial concerns? Were that the case, Christian life would be a kind of paradox. It would be unavoidably unhappy. We should all have to live in a continuous bad conscience. When turning to God, we should have to be reproaching ourselves for leaving the needs of our neighbor; and when attending to our neighbor, we should have to be blaming ourselves for not giving our attention to God.

Let us remark first of all that the idea that there are in our lives as it were two opposed poles, a human pole and a divine pole, is one that does not correspond, at all, to the actual biblical conception of man. On the contrary, the Bible reveals in man a magnificent unity. If an opposition exists, it does not exist on the plane of the objective reality of things, but on the plane of the deformation which we bring to it. We are torn, not between man and God, but between the glorification of God on the one side and idolatry of man on the other. It is clear that there cannot be two absolutes. Were there such, you would have inevitably either the impossibility of achieving unity or the necessity of choosing between the two. But in reality, in the truly Christian conception of man, this is not the case by any means.

We can attempt to appreciate this by inspiring ourselves particularly with those first chapters of the Bible which are like the charter of biblical anthropology. There we see in man three dimensions. The first is mastery of the world. When the first Adam was created, God brought the animals before him in order that he might name them and thus manifest his domination over the animal world. The Bible tells us also that he was placed in the Garden to cultivate it, and that everything was placed at his service. A first aspect of biblical man is therefore his terrestrial duty, that of acquiring mastery over the world in order to bring it into his service. Contrary to a prejudice which we meet around us, and that must be demolished forthwith, nothing is more conformable with the biblical vocation of man than the inventory of all the riches of the earth and the discovery of all its resources, for the purpose of making them serve personal development.

From this point of view, nothing seems more profoundly biblical nor more legitimate from the simple point of view of the faith than the prodigious progress man is making today in this investigation of the universe. It would be absurd for a Christian to be upset over this progress of science, to pout about it, and to fancy in it heaven knows what obscure menace to salvation. It would be an infantile Christianity indeed to fear that the faith might stand or fall with some new discovery; were our faith really in that case, a pretty flimsy thing it would be. Quite to the contrary, man's effort to discover the riches of this marvelous universe and to glorify God in his wonderful works is perfectly in line with our vocation. Let it be a Russian who first sets foot on the moon. His seeing in the accomplishment only a manifestation of human power will not keep him for all that from being the unwitting instrument of the designs of Providence.

A second aspect of man in the biblical conception is his bond with other people. That is what the Bible tells us: It is not good for man to be alone. And therefore God created Eve. It is noteworthy that in the second account of the creation of man, the one in Chapter II of Genesis, the creation of Eve is not put in relation with the problem of the perpetuation of the species, but in relation with the fact that it is not good that man should be alone. This shows that it is of the essence of human nature to enter into communion, which is to say that man is not made for solitude, but designed to share what he has with others. Of this, human love seems to be the pre-eminent expression—yet the pre-eminent one only. All human relationships are expressions of this basically social nature of man.

Granted all this, biblical man does have a third dimension. And that dimension is adoration. Man was created in the image of God, which is to say that, for one, he masters the world which is inferior to him; that, for another, he is to be in communion with his fellow-creatures, who are his equals; but that, finally, he must acknowledge the transcendence of what surpasses him. On one very fine page, Romano Guardini shows that the Bible rhythmically distributes man's life between work and adoration, with six days given him to master the world, and a seventh day given him to acknowledge the sovereignty of God.

That is constitutive of the very being of man. For us, man is someone who receives himself from God—and not only by some what shall we say? some initial twist of the wrist, but in a here-and-now relationship. At this moment, as I move my hand to write another word, I exist only inasmuch as God gives me to myself, and, so, for me, to exist is to be in relationship with Another; to be is to be two. Man's pretension to self-sufficiency, which is the basis of a certain existentialism, is an illusion. From the point of view of the Bible, it is in recognizing his dependence on God that he sees aright.

This relationship with God does not represent some kind of accessory truth, fitted on to a humanism which could exist substantially apart from it, but is constitutive of man as such. Hence a man who refuses to consider it, a man without adoration, is mutilated in his person. When we raise our voice today against every sort of atheistic humanism, whether this be marxist humanism or liberal humanism, it is not simply God that we are defending, but man himself. A man without God is not fully human. I am surprised that Christians are not better aware of the human stake in what they are defending.

The error of certain Christians has been to believe that work in the social field is enough for the fulfilment of their Christian duty. It is absolutely insufficient, for love of neighbor does not exhaust the Christian vocation; love of God is also an essential in it. The duty, hence, to work to maintain the presence of God in the midst of the world that is abuilding, in the universe of applied science, is plainly Christians' most essential task. This world, in its technological aspect, might strictly speaking be constructed without them. After all, engineers are being turned out like sausages in the "people's democracies," and chances are good that shortages tomorrow will not lie in that direction. The short supply that may well cause the pinch in machine civilization tomorrow will be in adoration.

I must make clear that this is not just a part of the individual's makeup, but of collective civilization. A city where you would look up and see only factory chimneys, and never a church spire, would be a hell. And we may ask ourselves whether, today, service to civilization may not lie even more, for a boy or girl, in going to the seminary or entering a convent than in going to work in a laboratory. And I mean from the simple point of view of tomorrow's civilization and of social service. For, once again, without adoration human society becomes a world where we gasp for breath. And that, in truth, is the menace that overhangs the world today.

These thoughts bring me to the painful one of how well man today acquits himself in one department of his vocation, the technological, but how inefficient he is in that other department, adoration. But dissociate the two, and where is your humanism? And here perhaps we touch upon one of the greatest tragedies of the world of today. What has made the West is surely not skin-color! There are no such things as superior races. The West owes its superiority to two things: scientific invention and Christianity. The tragedy of our day lies in the fact that the West has given the world its science without giving it its Christianity. But separated from Christianity, science is a deadly gift. Of this we are only too well aware. In giving this instrument to the world without giving it Christianity, we are giving it an instrument which it may not improbably some day use to serve ends no longer those of the real service of humanity.

But all this was on the theoretical plane. The practical problem is perhaps more difficult. From what I have just said, we may be convinced; it is always important to be convinced, for conviction is an essential element for action; we act with joy when we are really convinced, whereas uncertainty paralyzes us. But it remains none the less that action does pose problems for us, that as a matter of fact we do find our lives divided between the demands of terrestrial duties (duties every day more heavy, be they those of family or of professional life) and God's call in our ears to stay in contact and in union with him. The problem presented here is to fit our earthly duties into our religious faith, to acquire a religious sense of our work in the world. Does all that I am doing make any sense? Or, after all, when it comes down to it, is it not a disguised distraction from what ought to be my real occupation: praying, keeping myself close to God, remaining free for spiritual things?

The number one thing, then, is the fitting of our work in the world into our faith. In what way can such work be the expression of our faith? Oh, it is easy to see how it may be so in some lines. Family life is one of these. It is clear enough that the duties of the mother of a family, the bringing up of children, will consciously be the expression of a divine mission intrusted her by God, the accomplishment of an assignment carried out under his eyes. Again, the laws expressing God's will regarding human love, in all that concerns life in our homes, are normally known to us. Many a problem can arise today in this area. And yet such problems lie within a whole situation whose import seems evident to us.

Things become a good deal more difficult when it comes to professional life, to political life, and to international life. Here, the union of the two domains of faith and work in the world is much less clear. It may be wondered whether one of the principal shortcomings of contemporary Christianity has not been failure to make clear how what I shall call collective charity fits in with Christian life. I shall explain what I mean.

It is certain that one of the main features of the contemporary world is the fact that the expression of charity is no longer only individual. One cannot acquit one's self today of the duty of charity by dropping a coin into a blind man's cup or giving a sandwich to a tramp at the back door. In reality, charity is institutionalized, as we know, and practically it is on the level of our participation in institutional life that we are of effective service to others. One of the forms of charity is seeing to it that people have a home. Now it is plain that the answer to this problem does not consist in offering our den or a couch and some blankets to whoever comes in off the street. It consists in trying to work to solve the housing problem efficiently in its own sphere, and this naturally involves procedures of a nature not individual at all, but collective.

Charity operates more and more on this level. Now, it is extremely difficult for many Christians to make the connection between their Christian life and these different forms of activity, or indeed to see how these come from any requirement of Christianity in the first place. If I conduct my business, if I make it to the voting booth, does this kind of thing really correspond to any requirements of my Christianity? It seems more likely that I do them, say, to have something to do, or to make money. The matter is a serious one, for I am liable to set up two absolutely different departments in my life. In the one, everything relating to business life, to political activity, and so forth; in the other, a certain amount of practice of Christianity. I have to see, then, to what extent the former can stem in me basically, by being connected with the foundation of my existence, from the requirements of the Christianity I profess.

I should say that there are really three questions here. The first is the most clear cut. It is that my taking part in the workaday world is my fulfilment of a duty—is obedience, that is, to God, who requires my service to society. I recall having had this point wonderfully well cleared up for me by my reading of a contemporary Jewish philosopher, A. Neher. In a very fine book on the theology of the Covenant, he shows that, in the Old Testament, the prophets were continually imbroiled in political life. This is one of the biggest differences between the Old and New Testaments. In the New Testament Our Lord did absolutely no meddling in political problems. In the Old Testament, the prophets talked of nothing else. But Neher goes on to show that this did not come from the fact that—as Renan said, and as Marx said after him—the prophets were the voice in ancient societies of the struggle of the oppressed classes against the ownership classes.

In reality, for the prophets, political combat did not arise out of the class struggle, out of the revolt, that is, of the oppressed class against the oppressor class, but out of fidelity to the Covenant. The prophet's duty is to recall God's law to society as against all the infidelities which men are perpetually introducing into it. This duty, then, is to work to bring about the reign of justice, but justice in the biblical sense of the word, which is to say the law of God, which implies not only the establishment of just relationships among men, but also the recognition of the rights of God. Here we find under a new aspect the religious dimension of man's life.

There is in the second place the problem, and it is much more difficult, of the concrete expressions of this divine law. This is often the problem proposed in fact by Christians who do desire to serve in the social or political field, but who find that the Church at this moment leaves them strangely to themselves, being satisfied with furnishing some general views, without entering into the details of specific duties. To this one may reply first of all that what our world most lacks is precisely this reference to a conception of man, which is what the Church supplies by never ceasing to emphasize that there is such a thing as human nature. There are therefore laws of human love, of professional society, of political society which constitute the order established by God, to which every society must conform in order to be sound.

What constitutes the soundness of this natural order, so much disregarded by contemporary thought, but the importance of which we are increasingly rediscovering, is the fact that it is God's thought regarding man. We cannot, as so many men today think we can, make anything we like out of man. Man is not the creation of man, as Marx or Sartre have thought; we are not called on to invent a type of humanity; that has already been supplied, and what we have to do is to help bring it to fruition.

If that is settled, there remains the task, which is precisely that of laypeople, to apply this divine vision of man and of his destiny to particular concrete situations. Here is where there comes in that spirit of invention of which Jean Lacroix once spoke, or, to use a contemporary expression, what Gaston Berger called prospective, which consists in perpetually adapting the condition of man to the progress of technology. This is the great contemporary problem. For technology progresses, but it is indispensable to adapt its progress to human problems, without which adaptation technology will end by crushing man. Here, then, are admirable tasks, consisting in seeing to it that this creation of society is conformable to the laws of God.

There is another aspect of the presence of Christians in workaday undertakings. Up to this point, we have been talking above all about human nature in general, and of human nature constituted in part by its relationship to God. But it is obvious that in Christianity there is something more. In Christ there is revealed to us the final page of our destiny, which is not simply an earthly destiny. The uncreated Word of God himself came to seize upon our fragile human constitution to raise it up to the Father and to plunge it into the abysses of the life proper to him. Pascal said: "We know ourselves only through Jesus Christ." And true enough, it is only in Jesus Christ that there is revealed fully to us the mystery which we ourselves constitute.

Here, then, there is something more, which is not simply of the order of natural laws. The task of the Christian as regards earthly realities is to consecrate them—that is, to supply them with that ambient of grace within which alone they can reach their full development, finding in it health for their wounds and growth for their powers. This comes about through the sacraments. But the specific task of the laic in the Church is to be the agent who in a certain fashion turns upon the things of earth what is received by the grace of Christ. The function of the priest is to transmit this grace. And the function of the laic is to cause it to penetrate into all human things. This begins with the sacrament of marriage. It is in the climate of the grace of matrimony that human love, the love of man and woman, the love of children, has attained—in its own line—its finest delicacies and its greatest depths.

The same thing is true of other domains. It is in Christian grace that the human intelligence has reached its highest peaks. The more one studies the philosophy of India, the philosophy of ancient Greece, the thought of Islam, the more one is persuaded that, if it is in our West alone that certain truths have been attained, this is, as Gilson believes, because human reason has been aided by the grace of Christ's revelation without, and by the vivifying energies of the faith within. We need find this no source of pride, for it is not due to the quality of the Western mind, but to the fact that up to the present only in the West has intelligence been long bathed in the climate of grace. And in the measure that grace withdraws from the intelligence of the West, to that degree the West slips back into confusion of mind. It is one of the marvels of the grace of Christ that it draws human realities themselves—in their own line—to their natural perfection, independently of what it adds to them, by bringing them to surpass themselves.

I shall take another example. One of the things that most preoccupy me today is a certain abandonment of the treasure of Christian mores accumulated through the centuries of faith and formerly penetrating all of family life, social life, and in certain regards professional life. They were the result of a long and difficult conquest. We have the impression that today these—shall we call them Christian manners?—are in the process of being lost. For this reason I think there is no more magnificent undertaking, and especially for Christian women, than to work to re-establish ambients of Christian life. Human love, human understanding, and human work would find there, too, their full dignity and meaning.

But we must go further than all this. For if we stopped at what has been said so far, the question posed at the beginning of the chapter would remain unanswered: God would still be there on one side, and our work in the world on the other, whereas the problem is to determine whether we may not go to God through that work in the world. That is the question lying beneath all questions. I mean by this that if one could not approach God save apart from the workaday world, if work in the world were an obstacle to this approach, why then the situation we should face would be absurd. While God made us for himself, we should be spending our lives doing things that turned us away from him. The Creation would have been managed all wrong. And, in fact, do we not sometimes get the impression that things are all awry? Do we not feel that an incompatibility between the occupations which absorb us and a life of union with God does exist? So long as we reason thus, we are certainly in error. If there is one thing certain, it is that it is in our lives, just as they are, that we have to find God.

There is only one problem. Just one. And the problem is this one. All things were made to lead us to God. As a matter of fact, though, most things turn us away from him. The only puzzle to be solved is to make the things which turn us away from God become means to lead us to him. The whole question is right there. It is we, by the bad use we make of things, who render them blockades between him and us. There is therefore no other problem than to transform these very same things, the things that make up our daily lives, from obstacles into means. The whole of the spiritual life consists in nothing more nor less than this. The whole road of spiritual progress lies between the point where things are obstacles to the point where they have become means. And it is there, then, that our temporal activities, our work in the world, become the very material, we might say, for our practice of the spiritual life—means for going towards God. At that moment, we shall have caught on to the unity of our life. A day that can be spent in the most total banality, taken up by the purely human aspects of work, and bringing me in the evening only a kind of frightful void— it is up to me to transfigure it by a miracle of the heart and to invest it with a kind of incorruptible substance.

We must here push aside false problems and false pretexts.

We must rise above the level of purely intellectual difficulties. We must attain the real substance of the question. The truth about reality is the fact that our being is oriented towards God and must, on the level of awareness, make him out in and through all things. He lies hidden everywhere in our lives. We simply fail to discover him. I think of Peter Favre, the companion of St. Ignatius who had the marvelous gift of making all things, as he said, modes of prayer. "When you passed through mountains, fields, vineyards, modes of prayer presented themselves to you, consisting in asking for the growth and perfection of these resources. You gave thanks in the name of the owners, and asked pardon for those who failed to give thanks in spirit for these good things." There you have modes of prayer for a traveler. We can so easily allow our minds to wander here among useless and vain things, put down and pick up interminably a magazine or newspaper until we have read it through to the last want ad, and realize that we have passed our time stupidly. St. Ignatius' companion, in contrast, made the landscapes that passed before his eyes into modes of prayer.

This is where everything finally leads. Well we know that words and formulas are vain if they fail to reach the realm of conversion of heart and interior experience. Sometimes we are captivated by the ideas of those Hindus who seem to us to possess the secrets of I know not what arcane wisdom. But why search so far away, beyond the seas, when that wisdom is at our door—when it is, after all, up to us to find this peace. And this not in some kind of slipping away from our earthly tasks, but simply in a new view which we bring to bear upon them, the reflection that we have received them from God and are bearing them back to him. There is no other secret of existence; and this secret lies within our grasp.